Mary Ellen —
Thank you
for your friendship +
support!
Use your Power.

Love,
Vera
"Dr. G."

Your Power Belief System™

Change Your Life One Belief at a Time

By Vera A. Gonzales, Ph.D.

POWER PUBLICATIONS & PRODUCTIONS / LEAGUE CITY

The material contained in this book is not intended as medical advice. If you have a medical issue or illness, consult a qualified physician.

Published by Power Publications & Productions
201 Enterprise Ave., Ste. 600B
League City, TX 77573

Printed in USA by Instantpublisher.com
Cover and back design by Bookcovers.com

Hair & Makeup for Dr. Gonzales by Better Business Images,
League City, TX
Cover Photograph by Lakewood Photography, League City, TX
Printed on acid-free paper.

ISBN 0-9759571-1-2

To my father Armando E. Gonzales, a man who told me that I could do anything I wanted even though the world said I couldn't!

"The greatest revolution of our time is the knowledge that human beings, by changing the inner attitudes of their mind, can transform the outer aspects of their lives."

- William James

Table of Contents

Acknowledgments

Thank you to my mother who gave me unconditional love and support. Special thanks and love to my partner who always believed in me even when I didn't believe in myself!

Thank you to all of my family and friends for their undying support! Thank you to Cheryl Nowlin, Melissa Frala, and Dr. Heather Taylor for their assistance with publishing this book. Thanks to Dr. George Dempsey for helping me find my path!

Introduction

Are you living the life you truly want to live? Do you wish you could be more like the Jones' next door? Are you living with health difficulties? Do you live paycheck to paycheck? Is your work just something you do, not something you love to do? Have you bought into a blueprint that says this is how your life is supposed to be; this is all there is for me? What if there was a way to redraw the blueprint you are currently using into a blueprint for the life you want to have? What if there was a way to change your life into what you've always wanted it to be? I have struggled and have seen my clients struggle with the questions I just asked you. I have found a way to help myself and my clients gain access to a power that has changed our lives. This is a book about that power. This book outlines a technology that I am sure will help you in your life one way or another. It is a system that will help you see difficulties in your life as opportunities for power. This is a book about how your inner attitudes (thinking) affect your outer world (behaviors). By working with the fundamentals in this book you too can create change in your life and enable yourself to make choices of power and live the life you have always dreamed. I call this technology of change Your Power Belief System™.

    The concepts in this book are both new and ancient in origin. I have used resources from different spiritual and scientific philosophies that cross all ethnicities, nationalities, religious and spiritual beliefs. Its origins can be found in the philosophies of modern thinkers like Albert Ellis and Aaron Beck. This book describes a power and a gift that we were all born with and the different ways you can allow yourself to see and use this gift to create change in your life. And again, I am sure you will have a change in your life, but the change may come in a form you're not expecting. It may not come in the way you have been hoping, but it will come in the right way for you when you can define and start using your Power Belief System™.

Your Power Belief System™ is easy to read, and I believe that it will be beneficial to you and everyone in your life. It is important that you understand the fundamentals of the Power Belief System™ technology presented in the first two chapters. The remainder of the book builds on these fundamentals and deals with specific life areas that often cause people difficulty - relationships, prosperity, health, work and conflict. After you finish reading the book the first time, I suggest you go back and use it as a handbook for more specific problem areas.

I developed the technology in this book from my personal experiences, beliefs and attitudes as well as those of my clients and patients. This technology has helped many people change their lives. Over the years, I have been blessed to be able to work with many different people on different paths of life - from people perceived to be very successful and famous to people that were out of a job, unsuccessful and desperate to change their lives. The book talks briefly about these clients helped by the Power Belief System™. Of course, I have changed the names and some circumstances to protect their identity, but I think you will find it exciting to read about these wonderful people and how they have changed their lives.

Before we start, I would like to ask you to keep an open mind. The concepts in this book may challenge some of your current beliefs. Your ego may be a little bit resistant to accepting these concepts and making these changes - mine certainly was. Remember the fundamentals I am writing about have been around since the beginning of time. We use them every second of everyday! Unfortunately, we don't always use them to our benefit.

I believe now is the time to share this message with you. I hope you enjoy reading the book as much as I've enjoyed writing it for you. Take your time as you read the book. Try to understand the fundamentals, and accept them (make them your own). Then enjoy yourself because you are about to change your life and it will never be the same! You will live the life you were meant to live, and I know you will share this knowledge with all that you meet.

Live <u>your</u> dreams, no one else's!

"Conceiving, Believing, and Achieving = POWER"
Dr. "G"

1
POWER BELIEF SYSTEM™
THE BEGINNING

Belief Systems

What exactly is a belief system? A belief system is a set of thoughts, rules, attitudes, expectations and behaviors imbedded in your mind.   We use this structure of attitudes to make choices in our lives. Belief systems are created from our culture; from the knowledge and modeling we obtain from our parents, friends and perhaps from trial and error. Your belief system creates attitudes and behaviors (actions) that lead us to make certain choices.

For example, you may have been raised by parents who practice Catholicism. You may not have known WHY you were Catholic. When asked, you might have just said, "Because my parents are."   This is a common phenomenon. This belief you received from your parents that you are Catholic may have led you to an understanding and knowledge of Catholicism. You may have started to develop attitudes that were more in line with Catholicism, and you may have started making choices and performing actions based on these attitudes. For example, if you are a practicing Catholic you probably go to church and perhaps donate money to St. Jude. You make this donation because of your belief system. You may believe that something positive will happen from this donation.

Your belief system has created the tapes that are playing in your head. Belief systems (tapes) can be positive or negative or a combination of both. As a result, the tapes that play in your head can also be positive, negative or a combination. I believe the source of all of our difficulties in life stem from the quality of tapes we are playing. By quality, I mean positive or negative content. If we can change our belief system, and, therefore, those tapes, then we can make some radical changes in our lives. Once we become aware of the tapes that are playing in our heads and if they are not beneficial, we can remove them and replace them with positive, proactive ones that lead us to the life we want and are meant to lead!

Who has a belief system? Everyone does, whether you know it or not. We would not be able to move or make any choices at all if we did not have belief systems. I believe that we have one overarching belief system (life tape), and smaller sub-belief systems (specific tapes). So you may have a life tape playing, and that tape might cause one of your specific tapes to start playing in one of your sub-belief systems. (See Figure on next page.)

Is a belief system conscious? It is conscious to the extent that we are aware of it. I do believe that most of the time we react to our belief system and make choices almost unconsciously; so much so that we are not making choices at all. The choices have been hardwired by those tapes that we are playing in our heads! We don't know

2

why we are making certain choices in life. Many of us go through life asleep and unaware, almost like robots. When we make choices unaware of our belief system, our life is quite limited. Has this happened to you? For example some people present prejudice ideas against other people that they perceive as different. These ideas may come from their culture, family or maybe experienced through trial and error. Their belief system creates prejudicial attitudes that create the behaviors to make certain choices; like not associating with anyone who does not look like them, act like them, pray like them, etc.

LIFE TAPE

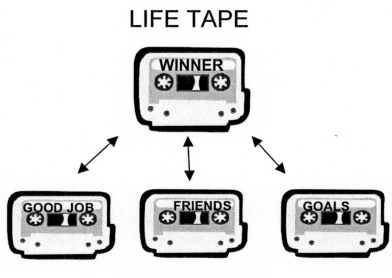

SPECIFIC TAPES

Is your belief system permanent? The structure of your belief system is permanent, but the content can absolutely change. You are only "locked" into a certain belief system if you want to be! This is the force and flexibility of the Power Belief System™ - change your belief system (thoughts, attitudes, expectations, rules, behaviors, choices) in any way you want.

A good example is a client I worked with that was severely abused as a child. This client had incorporated the abuse into her belief system, and she played tapes in her head that said, "Do not trust anyone because you will get hurt again." She came to see me because she perceived that she was not able to enter a romantic or friendly relationship with anyone. She did not want to open herself up to anyone because she knew she would get hurt. So she created the belief (attitudes, thoughts, expectations, and behaviors) of knowing up front that she was going to get hurt, and, by staying away from people that purportedly cared for her, she would be safe! She was making life choices based on this belief system.

So, how do you think this belief system was working for her? It worked exactly the way she set it up to work. No one wanted to be around her, and she made sure of it! It took some work on her part, but with help she was finally able to listen to the tapes she was playing and the inner talk she was having with herself. She was shocked. She had been sabotaging herself without even being aware of it! She began to realize that not everyone wanted to hurt her, and she started to open up to me and then to others. After working with her, she was able to record mental tapes for herself that were positive and action oriented. In a nutshell, this client experienced exactly what she created for herself, and now the experience was positive.

My Story

I am a licensed psychologist in the state of Texas. I did my training at a medical school in the southern part of Texas where my concentration was mainly in chronic pain and rehabilitation systems. Before that, I was a computer scientist for about 17 years. The irony of this long computer science career is that for most of my life I had always wanted to study psychology, but my inner voice told me I wouldn't succeed in psychology. The voice said that I should work in a profession where I could make money faster, so I could help my family because they were the most important thing in my life.

So that is exactly what I did. I listened to that voice in my head that said there was no way I could ever be successful and make money in psychology. I got my degree in computer science, and I went to work. Honestly, I can say that, from week one, I was absolutely miserable. Computer science was something that I did well; however, I was not doing what I loved or loving what I did. At times, I remember praying that I would be laid off; but I never allowed myself to think there could be something else. This was what I chose; there was no turning back; think of all the money my family had invested in my schooling, etc. I am sure some of you have felt this way as well.

5

Finally one day, I sat in front of the mirror and took a good look at myself. I realized that not only was I playing a tape (my inner voice) that said I could not succeed in psychology, but I was playing many different tapes- really negative tapes that said, "You cannot lose weight. You cannot be happy in a relationship. You cannot do this, and you cannot do that." So I decided right then that I was going to change at least one tape. I was going to allow myself to study psychology, and I did.

I resigned from my job in Dallas and found a job in Houston. I was accepted into graduate school and got my Master's degree in behavioral sciences (psychology). Most of my family and friends felt that my education would stop there. I would obtain a license to practice with a master's degree and just move on with my life. I had accomplished a huge goal, but I also had what Napoleon Hill referred to as a burning desire. I wanted to help people. I saw helping people as my life's work. I knew that to really help people, I would have to obtain a doctorate so I could become a licensed psychologist and have the credibility to work with different people. So this became my burning desire - I was going to get my Ph.D.

I started on that path and got accepted to a doctoral psychology program. During the program, the tape that had previously said I could not study psychology now began saying, "You will never finish." The tape would continue taunting me, saying:

- "Enjoy the time with your new friends."

- "Take all the courses and learn a whole lot, but you will never be able to finish."
- "You will never be able to do the research required."
- "You are not good at statistics."
- "You will certainly never be able to do a dissertation."
- "You are just not smart enough."
- "You cannot sit still long enough to write something so difficult."
- "It will not interest you."

This tape played most of the time I was in my doctoral program.

I learned during my training in psychology about Leon Festinger's cognitive dissonance theory, a phenomenon that refers to the distress felt when there is a discrepancy between what you already know or believe (current tapes that are playing) and new information or interpretation. For example, you may not like a co-worker but this co-worker may become a necessary ally for a project. You may then start telling yourself the co-worker is not that bad in order to reduce your cognitive dissonance. When there is an inconsistency (dissonance or conflict) between attitudes, behaviors, or opinions, something must change to eliminate the conflict. Your mind just cannot handle the conflict. It gets too upset. The mind gets anxious, and one of the attitudes, behaviors, or opinions has to win. Fortunately for me, the burning desire won. I actually finished the doctoral program and obtained my Ph.D.

I had many problems working against me during my program - my father passed away, my mother suffered a massive stroke, and I had to take an incomplete my second semester to take care of her. In the end, I was able to overcome those obstacles, change those negative tapes and replace them with new and stronger beliefs. I now know that it was the power of that burning desire (my beliefs) that drove me to my goal of getting my Ph.D. It was that power of believing in myself with every cell in my body that allowed me to complete those tasks. I began to see myself with my Ph.D. and achieving all of my goals, including caring for my mother. Most importantly, I FELT what it would be like to achieve my goals. I imagined every detail of finishing and defending my dissertation. I visualized myself presenting my research and answering any questions asked. I also visualized my dissertation committee congratulating me on successfully defending my work. When I did defend my dissertation, I was not even nervous because I had practiced (visualized and imagined) it in my head many times and was very prepared.

After recognizing the process I went through to get my Ph.D., and using the same process to help many of my clients achieve their goals, I realized I wanted to share this process with as many others as possible. This is how the Power Belief System™ began. By identifying your current belief system and changing any negative tapes you may be playing, you too can achieve your goals and live the life you want.

The Power of Chaos

Why does my life suck?

Why do I let things get so bad?

Why can't I make good decisions?

Are these questions you ask yourself? All three of these questions center on the message of this book. If these questions are playing inside your head, then your belief system is anything but powerful. In fact, it is destructive. Your belief system is creating patterns that put you into cycles of fear, cycles of blame and cycles of pain; however, it is easier to stay the same. Change is scary and perceived to be very uncertain most of the time. To initiate change we generally need something to "happen." I use the term "chaos" for the event that causes something to "happen."

Many people have defined and understood chaos as being a sense of disorganization and frenzy. However this isn't necessarily the case. If we look to different scientific disciplines for a definition, you will see chaos defined as a theory. The definition states that simple systems with simple laws can result in complex outcomes. What this means is that if we break down all outcomes perceived as complex, we will find simple rules (or beliefs) that determine behavior. Some "thing" is determining your behavior that is based on your belief system. Your goal is to determine this "thing."

An example is an overweight person who is starting to record a new tape containing one positive affirmation - "I am healthy." This affirmation will create the chaos (conflict) needed for the person to start "seeing" himself or herself as healthy and begin engaging in healthy behaviors (e.g. exercising, eating balanced meals, etc.) which will result in complex outcomes (e.g. weight loss, lower blood pressure, etc.). In a sense I am defining chaos as a movement, a shifting or something out of balance. Once we encounter this shifting, change is right around the corner.

Chaos can be "voluntary" or "involuntary". An example of voluntary chaos would be when you choose to start recording new tapes that initiate change and help you to create your Power Belief System™. Involuntary chaos is when some "thing" happens to you, and that "thing" forces you to initiate change. For example, suppose you have always wanted to be a paramedic, but you were not able to attend classes because of your work schedule. Then you receive notice that your hours have been reduced because of company reductions (involuntary chaos). You find that you now have some free time.

St. John of the Cross, a Spanish poet in the late 1500's, referred to this chaos and the change it initiates as "the dark night of the soul". If you are like many people, you cringe when you hear the word "chaos" and think it is synonymous with misery. The irony is the "misery" definition of chaos could not be further from the truth. Chaos is the only way to achieve movement, change and balance in your life.

Chaos has a language all its own, but we are unwilling to listen because we fear chaos. Our fears make us want to hide within ourselves and cut ourselves off from the world. It is easier to stay the same than to create change because change is scary and uncertain. Most importantly, our fears create a belief of helplessness.

A good example is a client I saw who was in an abusive relationship. She was repeatedly abused by her spouse but would never leave even though she had the resources (money, friends, and family) to do so. What she did not have was the inner resource of a Power Belief System™. She had a belief system (tapes) that said she deserved the abuse - based on previous learning and modeling in her life - and that she would never make it on her own! She was in a prison of fear, guilt, and pain with no plan for escaping.

When people like the woman above ask me why they cannot make decisions, my answer is always, "Because you believe you can't." You are making decisions and choices based on your current set of negative and destructive tapes. So, working the fundamental problem of changing the ineffective tapes that are playing in your head will lead you to change!

The bottom line is that it doesn't matter if you decide you are going to change your life and go back to school, lose weight, etc. Chaos has to happen for us to initiate and create change in our lives. It forces us to review our current tapes. If you have not changed your negative tapes, then you will still have a voice inside you saying "You are no good, etc." You will get exactly what those thoughts are loading into your brain. This is vital for you to understand. Your life may "suck" because you may be creating it to "suck" by allowing certain destructive tapes to play in your head and script your life!

Creating the Technology

I developed this technology because I had no other choice. I believe I was "called" to do this. It has been another burning desire of mine. I started to notice how I was communicating with and advising my clients. I began to notice patterns in my dialogues with clients that were both making and not making gains in therapy and coaching. When I studied these patterns, I found a complex weave of thoughts, inner voices, attitudes and rules that played a huge part in these clients making or not making positive changes in their lives. It all came down to their belief systems! I continued to refine this and began seeing how powerful my client's belief systems were. I also realized how fundamental the belief system is in creating change in a person's life. I found that belief systems are gateways to helping people, including myself, change their lives in an everlasting way! I saw my clients start to live the lives they were meant to live.

The Power Belief System™ technology is new, but the core basis has been around since the beginning of time. The most interesting part of this is that I did not know about any other resources at the time I was developing the technology. I was developing a knowledge structure based on my life and my work with clients. It was only after I developed the basis of the technology that I started researching different philosophies, spiritual teachings, and religions and found that technology is actually based in ancient knowledge. I think this is awesome. It is like I said before; I have been "called" or led to do this! I have threaded different parts of many sources together and have refined their application into the technology of the Power Belief System™.

One of the most powerful references I found that I think sums up the philosophy behind the Power Belief System™ is the following:

> *"Verily I say unto you, whosoever shall say unto this mountain, Be thou taken up and cast into the sea; and shall not doubt in his heart, but shall believe that what he saith cometh to pass; he shall have it."*
> Mark 11:23

That is a powerful statement that implies to me that NOTHING is impossible no matter how it is first perceived!

Look again at the quote I have in the beginning of the book by William James:

"The greatest revolution of our time is the knowledge that human beings, by changing the inner attitudes of their mind, can transform the outer aspects of their mind."

Here is a man, known to many as the father of psychology and modern thought that lived in the 1800's and made this statement. My interpretation of this quote is that we can change our *"inner attitudes"* (tapes playing in our heads) to create change in *"the outer aspects"* of our minds (our lives)! By changing the tapes in our head, we can create change in our physical lives! Can you see how powerful that is?

2

POWER BELIEF SYSTEM™
UNDERLYING PRINCIPLES

Why it All Works

Energy Attracts Like Energy

What I believe is simple, yet very powerful. I believe in everlasting energy, and I believe that we are all manifestations of that energy. Maybe you have referred to this energy in a spiritual way and think of it as a higher power. Perhaps you call this energy God, Spirit, Universe, Jesus, Mohammad or Buddha. It doesn't matter. It is all the same phenomena. It is all life. It is all energy along the same path.

What do we know about energy? We know that it can never die or end. This is a fact of science, and it is undisputable. So what does this really mean when we say that energy can never die or end? Think of a loved one who has died. The body may go away, but the person's energy (soul, mind, spirit) leaves behind a virtual signature of itself. We may still be able to "feel" them with us, and it is comforting. They are still with us, only in a different form. We can no longer describe them in terms of our limited language and physics. We are all the same at this very basic level. If you could break down this wholeness of our beings to the most indivisible level you would find a spark of energy and nothing more.

Everything on this earth is a spark of energy. The earth itself is a spark of energy. So we are all connected by the fact that we are all energy.

All energy vibrates at certain frequencies, most that we can measure. Have you ever gone into a place and said "I get bad vibes here" or "I'm getting bad vibes from that person?" Change your vibration (energy) and the vibrations (energies) around you will change. They will have no choice. You will get back what you give out in energy. Keep in mind that energy is everything and everything is energy. You will attract the same energy to you as you give out! Suppose you are walking in a mall and you frown at everyone. What do you think other people will do? They will probably frown or make an unfriendly face back at you! See how this works? It is important that you understand this principle.

The Brain Does Not Know the Difference Between Fact and Fiction

One of the most important and fascinating facts is that our brain does not know the difference between fact and fantasy! It does not know the difference between right and wrong. It does not know the difference between a penny and a million dollars. It is your belief system that assigns meaning and emotion to the information your brain receives, not your brain. If you are telling yourself a lot of negative stuff, your brain will produce negative stuff!

For example, what happens if you tell yourself the following?

• I can't do this.

16

- I have never succeeded.
- Mom and Dad said I would never amount to anything.
- I never could write well.
- I can't do math.
- I'm too fat.
- I'm too old.
- I don't have enough money.

Guess what you will get back? The same thing you put in! Your brain will just take "your negative stuff" and do everything it can to make sure the negative stuff happens; it knows no other way. If you say, "I'm no good" or "I can't do this", then your brain will do everything it can to manifest or create that reality for you. Understand? This is very powerful, and it is vital that you understand this principle.

What would happen if we changed the negative stuff and created positive stuff? Again, the brain does not care or know the difference.

"There is nothing either good or bad, but thinking makes it so." William Shakespeare, *Hamlet*

So if you are telling yourself "I am a successful person" or "I am CEO of a new company", and you really start to believe this and feel what this would be like, what is your brain going to do? It is going to try to do everything it can to lead you in the right direction of making choices and creating attitudes, expectations and behaviors to create a belief system that allows you to accomplish your goals. You now have a **Power** Belief System™ because you are talking to yourself in a positive and productive way and allowing this inner talk to lead you toward positive outcomes. You will be amazed at the changes in your life and all the rippling effects you will see from these changes.

So, you still do not believe me? You still do not believe that your brain does not know the difference between fact and fantasy? Here is the best example that I can give you; the most concrete example. There is a time in adolescence or pre-adolescence that both male and females experience a phenomenon. They will dream during the night and wake up in the morning with evidence of a physical expression that happened during the night. I am talking about nocturnal emissions, also known as wet dreams. Males and females will have dreams about engaging in sexual behavior and will have an external manifestation of an orgasm. There is nothing happening. There is no one in the bed with them, and there is nothing they are doing to themselves, yet there is that physical evidence of orgasm. So what is that all about? Your brain is receiving these thoughts or dreams (all energy) and producing an outcome as if the inputs your brain is receiving are true. They are to the brain! So, can you see how absolutely powerful this is! If it happens with nocturnal emissions, why can't you make it happen for everything else? You CAN and that is the miracle of the Power Belief System™. There is no reason you can't use this knowledge and create the life you want to lead!

Now of course, we did not always know the brain works the way it does. For a long time Descartes, one of the founders of modern philosophy in the 1600's, insisted that the mind and the body are split, and his beliefs perpetuated throughout the western world. We are only now starting to teach our future doctors about the mind-body connection. So, why is that? Why is it taking so long? What are we afraid of? Well, we are always afraid of change. That is a human quality. It takes a long time for new knowledge to enter into any organized structure and for it to get to a level that people integrate into their every day lives. Today when you walk into a bookstore, you see many books on the mind-body connection. We used to believe the body did one thing and the mind did another. But as you can now see, this is not the case. We do in fact have a mind-body connection and, even further, a mind-body-spirit connection. We will look at this more when we discuss how the Power Belief System™ applies to health in Chapter 6.

The Fundamentals

What does all this mean for you? How can you benefit from this? Well, you can benefit starting now! I think the first step is for you to understand the fundamentals of the Power Belief System™ described in the following sections.

Know Your Biases and Negative Thoughts

The Power Belief System™ is not hard to understand or use. However, you must be aware of your biases and negative thinking from the start. If you believe that you will get nothing from this book, then it will not disappoint you! You must allow yourself to acknowledge the concepts of the Power Belief System™ that may be new to you. Remember,

> *"If you think you can do a thing or think you can't do a thing, you're right."* Henry Ford

People can buy all kinds of self-help books these days. They can read them and put affirmations all over the wall; but if they do not believe these affirmations or even understand how to start believing them they will most likely fail. If you haven't slowed down and done the work necessary to find out what exactly you are telling yourself (you'll see how in Chapter 3) and under what conditions, then all the self-help books and affirmations are not going to work for you.

I know I said earlier that this technology is not hard to use, and it is not, but you must do some work. Only you can do it. You have to do some work because those beliefs that you have and those tapes that you are playing have been playing for a long time, and they are not going to give up that easily. They want to survive. Your whole being is used to these tapes! Anything else would mean that change is happening, and your being would have to accommodate and assimilate, and it doesn't like to do that. We prefer, all in all, that life remain the same.

Record New Tapes

Using positive thinking and positive affirmation is very powerful when you are performing them at the core level of your belief system. Positive affirmation is simply declaring something to be so even if it isn't true yet. For example, a positive affirmation might be, "I am a smart person" or "I am healthy." You are declaring something to be so! Some people have said that they have tried positive thinking and affirmations before, and they did not work. They ask how the Power Belief System™ is different. I would have to say that it is different because it looks at the fundamental (core) thoughts, attitudes, expectations, rules, behaviors and choices we are making and acts to change these core domains - our belief system. In other words, we are going to change the tapes that are playing in your head. Changing these tapes will move you in the right direction for you!

People that have not learned the technology of the Power Belief System™ may fail initially at changing their negative and useless tapes. Without knowing the fundamentals about change it would be easy to give up once those old tapes start fighting with you! This happens a lot because it is easier for us to stay the same. Change can be scary! We know how to load our brains with negative thoughts. Loading our brains with positive stuff, feeling good and having what we want in life may be new

21

experiences for us. But I am telling you that you are worth the investment to change your negative tapes!

Believe What You Record

I call the method of inputting data to our brains "loading." We do a good job of loading our brains with negative stuff. Now let's do an experiment. Start loading your brain with positive stuff! The more you focus on positive tapes, the more you will <u>believe</u> you can achieve the content of your tapes (your goals and dreams). But until you believe, "FAKE IT 'TILL YOU MAKE IT!" You will notice two things happen when you "fake it 'till you make it" - one, you will start believing what you are "faking" and, two, the brain has no choice but to process your requests and produce your outcomes. The more you believe and feel your dream to be true the faster it will happen. The problem is that those old tapes that are about to be erased or destroyed may start fighting for their lives! These tapes may start kicking off other tapes that may have been hidden to keep you off balance.

Power Belief Exercise

Try this experiment. Give yourself 21-30 days of loading your brain with the positive things that you want in life. Use "happiness" as an example. Just tell yourself, "I am a happy person. I have a happy life. I have a happy workplace." Notice how I am putting these affirmations in the present tense. This is important. Remember you will get what you ask for. If you affirm "I want to be happy" or

"I will be a happy person" you will get just that - a "wanting" to be happy and a "waiting" to be happy. You will be shocked and surprised at how well this experiment works. Because the bottom line is that your brain has no choice but to produce these positive outcomes. This is the power that you have available to you 24 hours a day, 7 days a week.

Summary

You have a belief system that comprises thoughts, rules, attitudes, expectation and behaviors that lead you to make choices in life. Your belief system creates tapes that are always playing in your head. These tapes can be positive, negative or a combination. The quality of tapes that you are playing will determine what choices you are making in life. These choices determine the overall quality of your life. In other words, if your tapes are negative, self-defeating and limiting, then so is your life! Chaos initiates change in our belief system and allows us the opportunity to discover what tapes we are playing and their effectiveness in our lives. By understanding the underlying principles of the Power Belief System™ - energy attracts like energy and the brain is unaware of what's real or not real – you can apply the fundamentals to create change in your life. The fundamentals of the Power Belief System™ - becoming aware of your biases and negative thinking, recording new tapes and believing what you record - will allow you to create a new life. A life that is empowering, non-limiting and positively affecting other people in your life!

Will this technology affect your self-image? Yes it will. You will definitely think differently about yourself. The truth of the matter is that if you were completely and totally happy with your life, you would not be reading this! So, yes, it will affect your self-image. It will help you to be the person that you are truly meant to be. It will help you to do what you were put here to do.

3

POWER BELIEF SYSTEM™
YOUR BLUEPRINT FOR LIFE

Steps for Creating Your Power Belief System ™ Blueprint

Step 1: Detecting Your Current Belief System

Before you can create your Power Belief System™, you must first identify your current belief system. Remember, your Power Belief System™ is your blueprint for the life you want to live. You are worth the investment of creating this blueprint. Some of what I will lead you through may be scary. You will be fighting your old tapes. If you feel a little scared in the beginning that is OK. Once you begin the process of creating your new belief system, you will immediately start to feel better and more positive, but this may feel a little "funny" to you at first. These may be new feelings. It's OK. Don't fight it. Go with the flow and watch what happens.

The following diagram may depict your current belief system and how it has been working for you.

Current Belief System

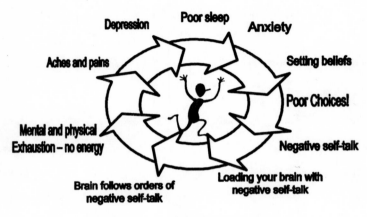

Depression   Poor sleep   Anxiety

Aches and pains   Setting beliefs

Poor Choices!

Mental and physical
Exhaustion – no energy   Negative self-talk

Brain follows orders of   Loading your brain with
negative self-talk   negative self-talk

Figure 1

The diagram is an excellent example of what happens to
you when destructive and ineffective tapes are playing in
your head. It depicts your brain following your negative
self-talk (tapes) and creating multiple "symptoms" of these
tapes. You are mentally and physically exhausted from
executing these tapes. You are not using your energy for
you. You are giving it away to focus on the circumstances
created by the tapes.

An example of this might be the way you handle
the stress of traffic. Suppose you are in traffic and
someone cuts you off before your exit. What does this do
to you? Following your current belief system, you may
allow this to make you angry and this may affect your
driving. Instead of just letting this go, you hold on to the
anger and all of your tapes associated with anger start to

play. You may start listening to a tape that describes all people driving cars like the one that cut you off as idiots. This may lead you to listen to another tape involving a similar incident where you got mad, and so on and so on.

Of course you are exhausted. You have given all your energy away. You may even give more energy away by retelling the incident to another person. When you become exhausted you experience more aches and pains. Certain hormones, enzymes and agents that reduce pain are dampened along with your immune system. This can lead to depression, insomnia and anxiety. All this time you are strengthening the negative beliefs in your current belief system. This, in turn, will lead you to make poor choices based on your current negative belief system. These poor choices create the opportunity for you to engage in more negative self-talk, which again loads your brain. Can you see the need to break this cycle?

What we will do now is define the process for you to determine your current belief system and then initiate chaos to create your Power Belief System™.

1. Learn to Relax. To detect your current belief system, you must first learn to relax and be with yourself. This may sound funny to you because you might tell me that you are with yourself all the time. Are you really? How many of us take the time to get to know ourselves and know why we think the way we do or what our beliefs are in certain situations. We usually do not. We usually just follow those old tapes without awareness!

Relaxation is a helpful way to gain awareness of your old tapes. You may already use a method for relaxation. If not, you can learn a relaxation technique easily. It doesn't matter what technique you use, as long as you are comfortable and feel grounded and safe with it. Some examples are meditation, visualization, deep breathing with stretching and progressive muscle relaxation.

2. Create your Safe Place. Using visualization, I would like you to imagine a time in your life when you felt safe and comfortable. Take your time doing this and be comfortable with whatever time in your life you choose. It may be a time from your childhood or a more recent time. It doesn't matter. In your mind, detail this place as much as you can. While you are going though your visualization ask yourself the following questions and write down your thoughts so you can refer to them later if you want to.

What does your place feel like? _____

_____

_____

Is there anyone there with you? _____ Who? _____

_____

Are you talking? _____ About what? _____

_____

_____

Are you laughing? _____ About what? _____

_____

_____

What do you smell? _____

_____

_____

Are you inside or outside? _____

What are you wearing? _____

_____

What are you hearing? _____

_____

_____

What colors do you see? _____

_____

Take all of this data and lock it in your mind and label it "my safe place." Remember the feeling you had while imagining this place and know that you can go here anytime you want to or need to. It is YOUR place! Now when you want to begin your relaxation, you can start in your safe place and then allow your mind to take you where it needs to go. If you start feeling bad, go back to your safe place. You will notice that you will start to feel better when you are in your safe place.

3. Continue Relaxing. Now allow yourself to use another relaxation technique to get even more relaxed. Any method that is comfortable will work. Some people love progressive relaxation, which is nothing more than just tensing and releasing different muscles in your body. The theory behind progressive relaxation is similar to the cognitive dissonance theory that I talked about in the beginning of the book - you cannot have a relaxed muscle and a tense muscle at the same time. So as you are tensing and releasing, you are relaxing. You can become an expert at this with practice and be able to relax deeply in any situation.

4. See Your Life as a Movie. The next step, I call the "movie screen" technique. Try to imagine yourself watching your life as you would a movie where you operate all the controls of the projector and screen. You are not going to have to relive or feel anything. You have total control of what you are watching. You can turn the movie on and off. You can stop it. You can pause. You can fast-forward. You can rewind. The images on the screen do not affect you as they did when you were physically there. You may have some feelings about the images you see like when you are watching a movie. There may be some sad parts and some happy parts, and you can share that with yourself. But you are totally safe, secure, and comfortable!

Allow different images to come up on the movie screen. For example, allow people who are different from you in some way to come up on the screen. Maybe they are of a different ethnicity, race, or skin tone. Maybe it is someone you know or work with. Maybe it is a stranger. Create different scenarios where you are communicating with this person and note what is happening to your body. Is it tense or relaxed? Are you able to make eye contact or do you divert your eyes? What are you thinking when this person starts an activity? What are you thinking when she or he drives a certain car? Wears certain clothes? Eats certain food? Do you get the idea? Keep going with this and make mental notes of everything or talk into a tape recorder. If you have difficulty seeing pictures in your head, try using pictures from a magazine to help you visualize. If you are still having trouble seeing pictures, then you might want to concentrate just on feelings. Always remember you have a safe place to go to if you start feeling uncomfortable.

5. Your Current Belief System is Revealed. I call this process of visualization and asking questions "inner visioning". What is going to end up happening is that you will start seeing all kinds of patterns start to emerge. You may find yourself saying "Oh my! I really say that to myself? I do that?" This process is remarkable, and you will start to see the things that you have been telling yourself. You may have had no idea you felt this way. I know, for me, the experience was just the most soul-awakening event I have ever gone through. It is scary at times because you have to face this stuff. So as you are going through this exercise and wondering is this really me, look at different parts of your life and assess how well things are going. Are you happy with how things are going?

I recall a client who would never have described himself as prejudice, come to that realization while he was going through the steps of identifying his current belief system. He realized that every time he saw someone who was of a different race or ethnicity than himself driving an expensive car, he would say to himself, "What are THEY doing driving that?" "How did THEY get that?" The tape shocked him. He realized he must have been playing this tape in other situations besides this one. He became aware that he might be making decisions at work or home based on his faulty belief system. He came to understand that he was not prejudice against anyone but himself. His negative thinking of others was just his own brain echoing tapes that he was playing about himself! This was a very powerful insight for him, and it was the chaos he needed to initiate change.

If you are happy with your beliefs about "different" people, then use inner visioning with another area of your life, like relationships, money, etc. Ask questions about each area of your life where you want to make improvements. Perhaps you are in a relationship, and during inner visioning you see yourself as not being comforting, comfortable or secure in your relationship. You notice that your jaw tenses and your eyes divert away from your partner. This is an indication of what your belief system is concerning your relationship and gives you the data on what tapes you need to find and look at. You may have a tape that says, "I am miserable in this relationship, but I know I'll never attract anybody else this good-looking, rich, intelligent, etc." During your inner visioning process you will start to see patterns in your life that have been based on your current belief system and all the ripple effects this has created in your life. You will be able to see all the tapes that need to be replaced with more powerful and positive ones that will lead you in the direction that you were meant to go in life.

Step 2: Voluntary Chaos

Now let's discuss the chaos you need to drive you towards your new Power Belief System™. Rather than wait for some outside force to cause the changes you need to move, follow the process below to create voluntary chaos.

1. Acknowledge that these negative tapes were in your life for a reason.

2. Thank them for what they have taught you and let them go.

3. Let yourself release the negative tapes by visualizing yourself burning them, releasing them on balloons, erasing them or pulling the tape out of the cassette deck.

4. Know the tapes can never harm anyone else.

5. The act of releasing the tapes is also one of forgiveness. While you release the tapes forgive yourself for any part you played in holding on to the negative tapes.

You no longer need this negativity in your life for any reason. Remember chaos is necessary for change. You are taking a proactive lead by initiating this chaos your self. Anytime you take the initiative to change your life, you are creating voluntary chaos.

You now have the data you need to identify your current belief system and you can initiate change (chaos). Now let's look at the steps necessary to create your Power Belief System™!

Step 3: Create Your Power Belief System™

Now let's talk about the nuts and bolts of this technology I call the Power Belief System™.

1. Replace Negative Thoughts with Positive Ones. Now that you have gone through the exercise of identifying your current belief system and creating voluntary chaos, you are aware when you are producing negative self-talk. When this happens, you simply change these tapes by loading your brain with positive, action-oriented, results producing self-talk. Your brain will follow these new tapes, and you will start to notice right away that you have more energy. Having more energy, you also notice that you have fewer aches, less pain, are in a better mood and are sleeping great. Your self-esteem is improving, and you are cementing your beliefs with these new positive feelings, attitudes, expectations, thoughts and behaviors. These new beliefs are leading you to make powerful choices! Can you see how this new cycle of your Power Belief System™ will be strengthened every time the cycle is completed? This is an incredible and miraculous

power you have! The diagram below depicts your new
Power Belief System™.

Power Belief System™

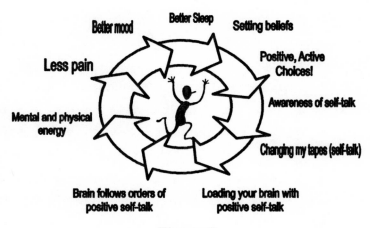

Figure 2

2. Believe. Remember, you may not always
believe what you are telling yourself in the initial phase of
creating your Power Belief System™ and that is OK. Do
you recall earlier when I talked about "Fake it 'till you
make it?" Let's look at this statement a little closer. What
I am saying to you is that if you can truly believe these
new tapes you are creating and you can "feel" and "see"
their outcomes, then this process of change will happen
soon for you. Most of us have to work a little harder,
because we do not believe the positive things we are telling

ourselves in the beginning. That is OK. You now know from learning this technology that the "believing" will happen. Remember, the brain has no other choice but to process your requests! The most remarkable thing is that your Power Belief System™ is a dynamic system that is self-fulfilling. What I mean is the more you load your brain with positive and productive tapes, the more you will come to believe the system works even if you did not believe in the beginning.

3. Visualize. The use of visualization can also speed things along for you. Imagine (visualize) in your mind what you want your outcomes in life to be. Perhaps one of your desired outcomes is to spend more time with your family. You might visualize yourself taking your family to the park for a picnic at noontime during the week. Let your mind take you where it wants to go. Maybe you visualize yourself becoming a better manager of your own time, completing tasks earlier than scheduled and freeing up the noon hour to spend with your family. Visualize as many details of the picnic as you can. What are you eating? Is the weather hot or pleasant? Once you start this process everything starts falling in place with your work, time management, other responsibilities, etc. It is amazing! Again, if you have trouble with visualization (pictures) then just use your feelings. It's all the same to the brain. It's all energy!

4. Let Yourself Feel. Allow yourself to FEEL the outcomes you want! If you are able to feel your desired outcomes, you are already experiencing them. Your brain then accepts this input as true and will start the work to get you to your desired outcome. You are telling your brain, "This is happening now. Get busy and create!" If you have trouble feeling the outcome initially, using "Fake it 'til you make it" will eventually produce the feeling as well. Try answering the following questions to help you identify your feelings:

What does the desired outcome feel like?

What are other people saying about your new life?

What emotions are you experiencing?

Step 4: Repeat as Necessary

You may need to repeat the method of identifying your current belief system so you can make sure you have identified all your negative tapes. You will then follow the process of releasing these negative tapes and recording new positive and productive tapes. Repeat this as many times as needed. Remember, some of those negative tapes are fighting to survive! Let yourself release the negative tapes by visualizing yourself burning them or releasing them on balloons. Thank the tapes for whatever lesson you have learned from them and know the negative tapes will harm no one else.

Your Power Belief Zone™

As you begin living your Power Believe System™, you will experience periods where you are totally focused, relaxed and experiencing peace in mind-body. You will be

37

completely aware of your tapes and "loadings" and how they are impacting your ability to get to your goals. You will be able to "re-load" positive tapes as necessary in order to attain your desired outcomes. I call these periods of awareness, your Power Belief Zone™.

When you are in your Power Belief Zone™ you will experience heightened awareness and creativity. Think of an athlete that we refer to as "in the zone." The athlete isn't necessarily consciously thinking about the things he does, but he can accomplish tremendous feats when in "the zone." You may also have experienced "the zone" at a wedding of someone you care for, the birth of a new baby, graduation or the achievement of a life goal. These events bring awesome feelings of power and joy. These feelings are something that you need to bring into your consciousness to help you center yourself and live in your Power Belief Zone™.

Summary

Detecting your current belief system allows you to see what negative tapes are playing in your head. It enables you to see where you need to strengthen some beliefs, let go of others and what areas require the recording of new tapes. By learning to relax and allowing your mind to take you where your need to go, you can use different techniques for identifying what needs to be changed. Once you start replacing your negative tapes with positive tapes, you will begin to immediate feel better. If you are having trouble believing your new tapes initially, then remember to "Fake it 'till you make it" until you do!

A Review

Following are the steps to creating your Power Belief System™

Step 1: Detect Your Current Belief System

1. Learn a relaxation technique and get comfortable being with yourself.
2. Create a "safe place" through visualization where you can start your relaxation or go to if you become too stressed.
3. Allow yourself to get into a deeper relaxation using any technique that is comfortable for you. Be prepared to have your subconscious reveal even more to you and remember it's OK to be shocked by this.
4. Use the "movie screen" technique when you are having trouble facing certain truths.
5. Start you inner visioning and be prepared to start hearing, feeling and seeing thoughts and things you are telling yourself and believing in.

Step 2: Voluntary Chaos

1. Acknowledge that for whatever reason you felt you needed to have negativity in your life, it is now gone.

2. Thank what you have learned from the experience and let it go.

3. Visualize the negativity as old cassette tapes that you will now burn or release into the sky on balloons.

4. Realize that these tapes will never harm anyone else and will disintegrate.

5. Forgive yourself for any part you may have played in holding on to the negativity in your life.

Step 3: Create Your New Power Belief System™

1. Every time you release a negative thought replace it with a positive one.

2. Believe your new positive thought or "Fake it 'till you make it."

3. Visualize yourself achieving just one outcome you desire.

4. Let yourself feel this with every sense you have and replay as often as you can.

Step 4: Repeat

Go through the same process until all negative thought has been replaced.

Now that you are armed with the fundamentals of this technology, let's see how we can apply it to difficulties you may be having in your life.

4

YOUR POWER BELIEF SYSTEM ™
AS IT APPLIES TO RELATIONSHIPS

*K*nowing what you know now after learning the fundamentals of the Power Belief System™, why do you think you have the relationships you have? Why do you think you attract the current people in your life? Like energy attracts like energy. You will get back what you give out. It's a simple idea, and yet we probably never think about it. People always ask me "Why do I pick the partners I do?" That's simple. I tell them, "You are attracting to you what you give out and what you think you deserve!" So why do we not give out things that we want to get back? You attract people that represent aspects of yourself that you don't like. This is a manifestation of your belief system. If you are telling yourself "I don't deserve to be treated well," then you will attract someone who will treat you poorly!

The same is true when we are critical of people or when we feel like it is necessary to talk about people because they are different from us in any way. Every time we feel like we have to make fun of someone, we are only making fun of ourselves because that person represents something about us that we do not like. Like energy attracts like energy! That person (that you criticize or have difficulties with) presses a button in you. Everyone has been in situations where you say, "They just press my buttons." Then you hear yourself say, "They made me feel this way or that way (angry, sad, etc.)." Well, that is impossible. Nobody can MAKE you feel any way. You do this to yourself. Remember energy is everything and everything is energy.

So to attract the right relationship for you, load your brain with the relationship you want. But what do you think you deserve? Do you deserve a good relationship, a healthy relationship full of communication, love, understanding and growth? Or, do you feel like you deserve nothing more than you have seen in your past relationships? Perhaps your parents did not model the best of relationships for you. Maybe they modeled for you something negative, something dysfunctional. Have you ever stopped to think that you may be repeating this over and again in the types of people you choose to associate with, even those people you work with? Who do you hang out with? Who makes you mad? Who makes you happy? Who do you just feel wonderful around - just the thought of that person makes you feel good - whether it is somebody that you know personally or admire from afar, even on TV? It doesn't matter. It's all energy. So what energy do you want to be around? That is what you need to find out, and that is what you need to load in your brain.

Find out what energy you want using the relaxation and visualization exercise from Chapter 3 (there is a summary at the end of the chapter). What attributes do you want in a person? You should know this because they are the same attributes you want for yourself. You want to load your brain up with the person you want to be. Remember that energy attracts energy, and guess what? You will attract the person that you want to be with. You will be "giving out" the energy you wish to attract!

You know, most of the time you get asked what kind of person you are looking for because your friends want to set you up. Most of the time your "soul mate" is nothing like what you describe to your friends, but your soul mate is the person you are supposed to be with. There is a match waiting out there. There is an energy, and if you were to fight that energy and say "Oh no, they need to be blonde, have this kind of body, be a doctor, etc.", then you will end up miserable because you would be denying the energy that you need to be with! You have to be in line with your core beliefs and see how those are hurting or helping you. Once you start loading your brain with positive and productive thoughts, you will start accepting what is yours to have. You will place square pegs in square holes, not round ones! You need to feel and believe in the changes that are happening. Remember that those old tapes will fight for their lives. You have to believe you will change and handle the fundamental problem of changing old, negative tapes. Otherwise, you can read all the books you want, do yoga or listen to self-help seminars, but you are just masking your problems. It is just like taking a pain pill. Unless you treat the problem of negative tapes, you might as well just take a pain pill.

Try this and prove it to yourself. It happens. It works. It is real. It is powerful, and here is the biggest prize. It is yours. It is within you. It has always been there waiting for you to wake up and be aware and USE this power! Use it for whatever you want. Create the relationship you want and need. You have gone through the fundamentals, and you have done the work, so you cannot go wrong. Because once you have that energy, then that person who is meant to be with you will be attracted to you. That person will come into your life, and it may be something unexpected.

This technology is not just for romantic relationships, but for any relationship. A relationship is a relationship, energy is energy! You manage and mismanage your relationships for the reasons I have been discussing. You might have had something modeled for you that you decided to copy without really considering if it was right for you. You did not have a Power Belief System™ at the time. You did not take the time to know yourself, and you were managing your relationships the only way you knew, through a negative blueprint. These bad relationships are what you created and wanted for yourself. Are you saying to yourself that this is not true? You don't want bad relationships? Then why do you keep repeating the same cycles? Even though you have not sat down and actually said to yourself "I want bad

44

relationships", it's true because these bad relationships keep repeating over and over in your life.

So in general, your belief system affects your relationship-seeking behavior by creating the attitudes, expectations, rules, thoughts and behaviors (tapes) that lead you to make choices based on these tapes that you have playing in your head. Your Power Belief System™ will allow you to become aware of anything you may be doing to sabotage yourself and, thus, your relationships. It will allow you to become aware of your relationship avoidance behaviors. There are many people who say that all they want is this-or-that relationship to be happy. We have all heard this from people, right? The irony is that these people do everything in the world to avoid relationships. They are not willing to take chances to meet new people. They are not willing to see things outside this perceived perfect person that they have in their head. So they have limited themselves and have missed many chances to meet people that could have had a positive affect in their lives.

Your Power Belief System™ affects your willingness to be successful in relationships. You are confident and more willing to take chances. You are more willing to do things that you normally would not do because you now load your brain with positive and productive thoughts. Your brain has no choice; it has to manifest this just like it has been manifesting your negative thoughts! You also find that you are more willing to listen to advice from

45

people who have relationships that you admire. You are looking at life though different "lenses" than before. You no longer tell yourself that whatever (negative) relationship (situation, etc.) you have is OK, and it was what you were looking to experience. You do not settle anymore! You are no longer afraid that you will never find anything else; you now know that is not a reality for you! You no longer say to yourself "I'll go ahead and just take this even though it is not exactly what I want".

So what do you tell yourself about achieving true relationships? Do you deserve a true relationship? You might say, "Yeah, of course, I deserve this. I am a good person, I work hard, etc." Take a look at the relationships you have had. Again, they do not necessarily have to be romantic. Are you living the life that you want to live with regard to your relationships? If not, consider what makes you uncomfortable about having relationships? Is there a tape playing in your head that says it is okay to have superficial relationships because they never work out?

- Mom and Dad's relationship never worked out.
- My grandparents' relationship never worked out.
- My uncle's marriage never worked out.
- My friends' relationships never work out.
- My business relationships do not work out.

Are those the tapes playing in your head? Then knowing what you know now, how in the world are you going to achieve this relationship that you say you want? You will not! Those negative tapes do nothing but sabotage you and keep you repeating cycles of negativity and self-destruction. You are going around in circles and your brain has no choice but to produce for you exactly what you are asking it to do. Why would you go through the trouble of developing a mindset that ensures negative results? Well, let's see - how about survival? You are protecting yourself from perceived pain. You are basing your actions on your faulty belief system! In using your Power Belief System™, you are developing a mindset that will ensure positive results.

Sabotaging behaviors are not readily available to you when you have created your Power Belief System™. You now have a system for positive input and positive results. You do not lose energy by loading your brain with destructive thoughts. You have the ability to load you brain with positive thoughts that lead you to positive choices and outcomes. When you are aware of the sabotaging behaviors of another person, you will no longer be attracted to that person. You will be a model for how life is meant to be lived! You are now vibrating at a higher frequency and attracting people of the same frequency or higher! Anything other than this could reduce your energy after extended periods of time. Listen to yourself and your body, and re-energize when you need to. Have you ever been with someone that just exudes negativity? It almost feels like it is covering you up like a thick tar. You will feel this very quickly when you begin living your

Power Belief System™, and you will be able to avoid these people.

Power Belief Exercise

Now let me give you the steps to a quick re-energizer and pick-me-up that you can use anywhere and anytime. Visualize yourself getting ready to take a shower with your clothes on. You are walking to the shower, and it is difficult because your clothes and body are weighted down with a heavy, black, tar-like substance. This substance is representative of all the negativity, depression, anxiety, anger, etc. that you are being exposed to, and it is weighing you down. Turn on the shower and notice how beautiful the water is. It is glistening and almost golden in color. Step in the shower and let this beautiful, energizing water flow over your head and body. You begin to notice that all of the tar-like substance is going down the drain easily to a place that will harm no one else. You also begin to realize that this substance (feelings, etc.) cannot be replaced. It is gone forever. As the tar starts to come off, you start feeling refreshed and energized. When all of this substance is gone down the drain, you step out of the shower feeling renewed! I use this exercise all the time during the day for an energy boost. It's wonderful! Use positive and powerful affirmations such as:

"I have wonderful people in my life."

"I have healthy relationships."

Don't use

"I will never get into a bad relationship again."

"I will not date as many losers as before."

Can you see the difference? Be very positive and state the affirmation as <u>fact</u>!

Pitfalls

What pitfalls should you anticipate when you are in the beginning stages of creating and using your Power Belief System™? In the beginning it is easy to get off track. Remember I told you that your old tapes would fight and use every trick they know? It is easy for us to just say, "What the heck. I know how to be miserable. I'll just go back to that." This is especially true when you are finding yourself spending a lot of time in negative and destructive situations or with people who are vibrating with low energy. Don't fall for these manipulations. You will be the victor in the end, and you are worth the investment of creating your Power Belief System™. Visualize your safe place and reaffirm why you need your life to change. Use the shower exercise in the last section to re-energize and focus.

If you stay aware of your thoughts, you will know right away when you are straying off track. Are you starting to settle? Are you questioning yourself about everything? You are aware and awake now, so go back to the fundamentals and get back on track! There might have been an old sub-specific tape that was left in your belief system, and it has started to play under a situation of stress, illness, having to be around low energy people, etc. Remember you have "done" negative, and it got you nowhere! The process of replacing your tapes will get easier the longer you use your Power Belief System™. You will see the negative tapes gearing up to play, and you will be able to turn things around quickly.

I love to tell the story of a client that was having some of the same difficulties with relationships I just described. He was a successful businessman and was quite happy with his life using his Power Belief System™. He received a call from a relative that asked him to come and see his mother because she had been in an accident and was convalescing at her home. This client had been estranged from his mother for some time. She had created a very negative life for herself and used her son as her scapegoat for everything, but he had been using his Power Belief System™ for some time now and felt that he was strong enough to go and be with his mother. He told me that he had not seen her in several years. The first thing she said to him when he walked through the door was, "Don't slam the door." He greeted her and wanted to hug her. She said that he was sweaty and stinky. He told me that during his visit, tapes that he thought he had burned were starting to play. He said one time he looked in the mirror and saw himself as a little boy.

He remembered the shower pick-me–up and started to visualize himself covered with a tar-like substance and went through the exercise. While he was visualizing the shower, it occurred to him that, when he was creating his Power Belief System™, he had mentally removed the safety tab on his tapes so they could not be recorded over. Knowing this gave him a sense of power and the knowledge that he was in a temporary situation. He was still strong. He also imagined a bubble of protection around him that protected him even further from his mother's negativity. He told me that, at that point in time, he understood his mother to be a person who was suffering inside. She probably had been for most of her life. Every time his mother would fire off a negative saying to him, he would just let it bounce off his protective bubble and end right back at its source, his mother. He finally realized that everything his mother was saying to him was really about her.

Refusing to give in to his mother's negativity and allowing himself to vibrate at the same high frequency he always did, a remarkable change was taking place. He told me that his mother would open her mouth to say something and then say, "Oh, never mind." He noticed that she became quieter, and, by the end of his stay, he was actually having a conversation with her. He could not ever remember a time when this happened before. When it was time for him to leave, he said that his mother even made some attempt at a good-bye gesture and whispered to him to come back. That story just solidifies how powerful we, as humans, are and how, by changing our inner attitudes, we can create change in our outer environments!

51

Remember that relationships are relationships, personal or otherwise. Everything you do to create and maintain your Power Belief System™ will create overflow and spill into other areas of your life.

5

YOUR POWER BELIEF SYSTEM™
AS IT APPLIES TO PROSPERITY

Prosperity is an interesting subject because we go through most of our lives wanting prosperity (usually equated with wealth), yet we sabotage our efforts to make it happen. Much like our personal relationships, we have a relationship with money. You may ask yourself "Why is everyone else prosperous but me?" It only appears to you that everyone else is successful and enjoying prosperity, and you're not. The truth is that you have the power to create prosperity. It's the same power that I've been talking about throughout this book. Energy is everything and everything is energy! So why would prosperity, wealth or success be different? Like energy attracts like energy.

Before we go any further, I need you to ask yourself what prosperity means to you. Is it wealth? Is it having "enough" money? How much is "enough"? Didn't your responsibility and expenses increase with your salary? So, how much money and things are enough for you to feel prosperous? Are you the kind of person that says "If I could just win the lottery or make x number of dollars a year, all my problems would disappear?" Does prosperity to you mean freedom and no limits in life? When you fantasize about having money, do you start to worry how to protect it, invest it or spend it? If so, that doesn't sound like freedom to me. Your definition of prosperity is important because it lets you know what tapes you are playing about prosperity.

I define prosperity as having what you want and need when you want and need it! Prosperity comprises several factors like money, friends, things, etc. How we define this is related to how we are defining ourselves. If you want to attract things (energy) to you, then you need to act as if you already have them. Acting ("Fake it 'till you make it") creates the energy you are wishing to attract. Acting allows your brain to be loaded as if an event is actually happening, which will set your beliefs and allow change to manifest. If you want money, ask yourself what someone with money acts like. What do they do? What do they talk about?

Be honest with yourself and find out how you really feel about achieving prosperity. Is there some tape that is still playing and stopping you from being prosperous? What tapes are you playing about prosperity? Would you define your family of origin as prosperous? Would your family perceive you as being "snooty" if you were prosperous? What do you tell yourself about wealth? What affirmations are you using? Again, are you creating a <u>lack</u>? Are you creating a state of <u>want</u>? If you are begging for money or things, you are focusing your energy on what you <u>don't</u> have as opposed to what you <u>do</u> have, and you will create nothing more than a sense of want and need. Your brain will follow your orders to the letter!

Why do you manage your money the way you do? You are managing your money according to the blueprint (belief system) that you have in your head. You've still got a limiting (negative) tape running in a loop that is stuck! It's so imbedded in you that you don't even realize it's playing. So get back to the fundamentals of Your Power Belief System™ (Chapters 2 and 3). Think about how your belief system affects your wealth-seeking behavior. You may have a belief system that is playing tapes that say "I'll never make more than $X a year because I am at a ceiling, and no one has ever broken through."

A client came to see me a few years ago that was having difficulty accepting the money that she had earned. She was a successful person and was perceived as such by her colleagues and friends. She had a straight path to the top of the company if that's where she wanted to go. However, the problem she had was that she was making more money than her father ever made in his whole 30-year career. She was playing tapes that said she shouldn't be making more than her father. It was almost as if it was disrespectful to him. Her tapes told her that her family would think she was snooty because of the things she would be able to buy, etc. This was a tape that she had loaded when she was younger under some circumstances she could not remember because her parents never acted in any way that would lead her to this belief. So she had a conflict. She knew that she had the skills and the ability to go where she wanted to go because she could see herself at the top. This is what she wanted. But then she experienced the following cognitive dissonance. "If I am at the top, I'll be making a lot of money and that doesn't mesh with these tapes I'm playing!"

She began to use the fundamentals from Chapters 2 and 3 to create her Power Belief System™. She began to realize what self-talk was going on and how it was limiting her in many ways. This realization was the voluntary chaos she needed to initiate and create change. She began to believe that she could achieve success beyond her wildest dreams and that it was OK to earn more than her father. In fact she began to load her brain with the thought that it was actually a compliment to her father and mother that she was so successful. When she got a position making six figures and got her first paycheck, she came to see me and said "I never thought in a million years that I would be making this kind of money at my age." She now believed that this was just the beginning. Everything in this woman's life changed. There were other things she was telling herself that she just didn't admit (remember how one tape leads to another tape, spilling over). She started losing weight, she started toning up, and she started standing up for herself. What she feared most from her family (thinking she was snooty) never came to pass. In fact, just the opposite happened. She became a role model for younger family members. Family members who never considered going to college were asking her opinion on the matter! It was a change in her total being that was just absolutely marvelous.

So are you willing to be successful? Are you willing to achieve prosperity? Wealth? People will say, "Oh yeah, that's no problem. I want that." But, everything about them, everything they do, every opportunity they deny themselves tells me that this is not true. They continue to sabotage themselves. Are you willing to listen to people that have achieved success? Are you willing to listen to people that have knowledge of how to be prosperous? Andrew Carnegie often said that he knew nothing about the process of making steel, but he surrounded himself with people that did! It's all about energy attracting like energy. Surround yourself with people that have done what you want to do. They are not going to vibrate at your energy level; you will start vibrating at theirs! Energy flows from low to high. Sabotaging behaviors and not believing in yourself are low energy behaviors. Believing and telling yourself that you can achieve the things you want in life are high energy behaviors.

Power Belief Exercise

To jump-start the process use the "Fake it 'till you make it" philosophy. Allow yourself to believe that you are already prosperous and act as if it were so. Allowing means conceiving it, believing it and feeling it. You could post affirmations all over the house - "I am a millionaire" or "I am prosperous" - but, if you don't believe it or feel it, these affirmations are simply pieces of paper with ink on them.

Try this exercise to help you see the "Fake it 'till you make it" philosophy in action. Visualize a purchase you would like to make that is financially out of your immediate reach, for example, a designer handbag or wallet that you have been wanting. Use a comfortable method to relax and picture yourself making this purchase. See yourself paying with cash. See yourself counting out the money to the clerk and leaving the store with your new bag. Ask yourself how you feel.

Are you happy?

Are you proud?

How does the bag or wallet feel in your hands?

What will you put in the bag or wallet?

Take out the receipt and note that it says paid in full. Now get a piece of paper and make a receipt with the store name, the bag or wallet name and the price of the good. Write on the receipt PAID IN FULL – CASH. Allow yourself to feel what the bag or wallet feels like in your hand and how you will feel when you carry it. Look at the receipt as often as you can and KNOW and BELIEVE that you already have the bag or wallet in your possession. Don't concern yourself with the HOW; just KNOW that you already own the bag or wallet. Anytime you feel that you are struggling with owning the bag or wallet, relax and see where these feelings are coming from. Use the energizing shower exercise (Chapter 4) to release any negativity or guilt that you have over owning this product. Notice what your body is doing when you visualize yourself holding the item. You will be surprised at how this item, or one better, will come into your possession.

Pitfalls

I know I said the brain doesn't know the difference between reality and fantasy and doesn't have emotion. So why do I need to believe it or feel it, you ask? If you can feel and believe upfront, your visualizations are clearer, and results will happen more rapidly. Your energy vibrations will match what you are trying to create and attract. Remember that although you don't have to believe in what you are loading in your brain in the beginning, your brain will eventually lead you to believe. Your brain is still playing negative tapes against these new loadings and affirmations, and it will slow down your outcomes; sometimes to what appears as a dead halt! That is why it is so important for you to do the upfront work of realizing what negative tapes you are playing so you can change them and start believing in what you are loading and affirming. Do not develop a mindset that would not ensure prosperity.

In order to change your tapes you have to disclose them. I am not talking about sitting down and talking to someone about it. I'm talking about sitting down with yourself and talking about it. We try to fool ourselves. We're in denial. We think that everything's okay. We do not want to believe that we may be sabotaging our

59

prosperity or anything else. That's hard to hear, but it's true. What do you tell yourself about achieving true prosperity? Wealth? Do you really think it's possible for you to achieve true wealth? Do you have supportive people around you, or do they laugh at your ideas? You have to surround yourself with the energy that you want to attract.

The method of creating your Power Belief System™ is a dynamic process that will be going on in our lives. We have to continue to be aware of the limiting and negative thoughts we are loading into our brains. We have to clean house once in a while. You will notice as you get more comfortable and start producing your desired outcomes that you won't have to clean house that often. You must remain aware of your thoughts because it is easy for some of us to go back to our old ways of thinking and behaving - it's the way we are wired. I wish this weren't true. I wish we could do this once and for all and never have to worry about it again. For the most part we can, but we always have to be aware of our loadings that may trigger old tapes that we thought were gone. I learned this the hard way and I would like to share my realization with you.

At the time I bought my first BMW, the car symbolized many things to me. It symbolized prosperity, success and how a person from a lower middle class family can achieve anything! One morning I went through a drive-thru that I go to often for coffee. The same woman usually waits on me. The first time I drove up in my new car she looked at me and said "What are you doing driving that car?" I said, "Oh, I just bought it, and I am really happy with it". When I left I started loading my brain with what I thought she meant. I thought she was questioning my right to be driving that car. I became upset. The next time I drove through, she looked at me and said "BMW, Big Mexican Woman". I gave her my order, and I left. What she said troubled me. I started wondering why she would say such a cruel comment. Being a large Hispanic woman herself, why would she have made that comment?

I began my relaxation and started realizing what was going on and what tapes I was still playing in my head. There were many tapes of shame and fear that were playing that I had as a child and adolescent. I went back to a time when I was made aware, by cruel comments, that I was not like the rest of the kids in my school. I looked different. My last name was different. I didn't live in a big new house, and my parents were much older than the other kids' parents. I went to an elementary, middle, and high school with few Hispanic classmates and no African-American classmates.

I became painfully aware of the negative thoughts I was telling myself and started to release these tapes and replace them with stronger ones of wholeness and pride. I didn't realize that I still had tapes like those until that woman at the drive-thru made those comments. Of course being a psychologist, I felt a need to have a meeting with her and discuss her comments. Fortunately, I didn't have to because the next time I saw her, she told me what she had meant. The funniest thing was this woman had said "Big Mexican Woman" not because she was referring to me being fat or not worthy of my car, but because she was calling me successful. She was referring to me being a "big time successful woman." She then went on to tell me that it makes her feel good when she sees me driving my car because it gives her hope of a better life for her children! Imagine that! I was totally shocked that I had allowed myself to overreact and begin playing the negative tapes in my head. This woman's comments were the chaos that I needed to re-examine my tapes and change them! This happens to all of us, and we have to be willing to continue to fight old tapes until the last ones are gone or at least not as powerful as before.

6

YOUR POWER BELIEF SYSTEM™
AS IT APPLIES TO HEALTH

Your belief system is the mind-body connection that you hear and read about from all different medias. I mentioned earlier in the book that western medicine is still in it's infancy regarding the mind-body connection and its affect on our health in general. We now have cardiologists that are telling their patients to get help for anxiety and depression because it could prove troublesome for someone already experiencing heart problems. Certain ailments of the heart can also create symptoms of anxiety and depression. Anxiety and depression are common in people who have unstable angina, tachycardia and sinus node problems. Gastroenterologists are advising patients to lower their stress levels because a body that is in stress all the time will produce too much of certain enzymes and not enough of others. The resulting imbalance can produce gastric distress. Orthopedic surgeons and pain specialists now know the importance of a psychological consult before invasive procedures and how psychological pain management is vital to a patient's recovery.

The thing that I want to stress in this chapter is the power of creating and executing choice and control concerning your health. I believe that you have control over your health when you are using your Power Belief System™. When you are in your Power Belief Zone™ and aware of what you are loading into your brain, you have control over everything! You decide what choices you will make to move your life forward based on this powerful blueprint you have available to you 24 hours a day, 7 days a week. Always remember, energy is everything and everything is energy. Thoughts, choices, expectations and outcomes are energy. We attract what we give out, and we give out what we attract! If our belief system leads us to make certain choices that produce certain outcomes in other parts of our lives, why would this not be true about our health? Remember that health is also energy, as is sickness.

I can recall several times when a colleague and I were working in a clinic where just about every patient and worker was sick with the flu. Everyone was either going home or calling in sick. I remember a favorite professor of mine approached me, sneezing and hacking while she was walking. I went to hug her and she said, "Be careful. I'm contagious, and you'll get sick too." I replied "Don't be silly! I don't have the time to get sick. I'm defending my dissertation next week. I'll be sick after that!" Guess What? That is exactly what happened. I defended my dissertation and was on cloud nine one day. I woke up the next day with the worst case of the flu!

A similar event happened to my colleague in the same clinic. She went up to introduce herself to a patient, and the patient said, "Careful I don't want you to catch this." She replied with, "I won't get sick. I only have three weeks left on my residency. I'll let myself collapse then." You guessed it. The day after her residency ended she became sick. We both had the belief (expectation) that we would remain healthy as long as we "needed" to be healthy.

Now let's look at two domains of health where I concentrate my studies, practice and research. The first is generalized stress and the other is chronic pain.

Generalized Stress

Numerous studies have found correlations (patterns) between illness and stressors. Illnesses from the common cold to cancer can be reduced to some emotional stress that plays a huge part in the illness! It makes sense that if we do not take care of whatever is stressing us, it will take care of us! Knowing what we know, it could not be any other way. Various sources, most notably the American Institute of Stress, estimate that 75-90 percent of all visits to your primary care physician are for some stress-related complaint or disorder. We now know that stress is a link in creating or worsening symptoms of all kinds of diseases including diabetes mellitus, heart disease, cancer, lung ailments and cirrhosis. Stress is also a link in a majority of accidents and suicides. More people than you can imagine are absent on an average workday because of stress-related complaints, including burnout.

What is Stress?

Stress is really any change you must adapt to. Stress can range from extreme negative to extreme positive. For example, extreme negative stress might be some type of danger like someone coming at you with a knife while you are trying to get in your car. Extreme positive stress may be achieving some life goal like getting a promotion to a level you never thought you would reach or being told you are cancer free! Many times people do not recognize stress in their lives (negative or positive). Of course, if you do not recognize it, you can't do anything about it. Look at the list below and decide which events are stressful and which are not.

- Receiving a work promotion
- Running out of gas
- Looking for a new home or apartment
- Your pet getting sick
- Your new office furniture delivery
- Meeting someone new
- Leaving for vacation

Well, all of these are stressful because all require that you adapt. Although there are many theories of stress, I maintain that everything comes down to our belief system. Whether the stress is environmental, social or physiological, it is still your thoughts, rules, attitudes, expectations and behaviors (belief system tapes) that create your perception of stress. Hans Seyle, a pioneer in stress research, said that it is not stress that kills us. It is our reaction to it.

A metaphor I like to use when describing varying levels of stress is what I call "rubber band" stress. Imagine you are standing in the middle of a large rubber band attached to your waist. This rubber band has enough slack in it to expand and stretch when you experience and adapt to stressful life events. For example, you have a new baby and the rubber band stretches to accommodate this. It then goes back to its normal state when you have learned how to adjust to the changes a baby brings. Another example is losing your spouse or child. Both of these are horrific events in your life. Your rubber band will stretch to its maximum and eventually come back to its normal state. What happens though if you have several rubber band incidents at one time or fairly close together? Stressors keep happening in your life that do not allow the rubber band to return to its normal state. What happens is that your rubber band will break, leaving you in a nearly constant state of stress!

Not all stress is bad, however. We all must experience some stress to stay alive. Our bodies are always adapting to some change. There are different stressors that keep our heart pumping and blood flowing through our veins. So I am going to use the term "beyond stress" to mean stress that is beyond what is considered "normal" for our well-being. Some of the things that happen to us when we are beyond stress are hives, allergies, cold hands and feet, shortness of breath and a reduced immune system that causes more colds. We can also have gastrointestinal problems, indigestion, constipation, Irritable Bowel Syndrome (IBS), musculoskeletal problems, low back pain, tension, headaches, spasms, aches and pains, cardiovascular problems, high blood pressure, irregular heartbeat and even hardening of the arteries.

When we are depressed, we lack motivation, our appetite changes and we can have more crying spells. We really begin to concentrate on those negative tapes that are playing. This can create anxiety, sleep problems and issues with pain and depression. Sometimes we even try to medicate ourselves with alcohol, food, sex, gambling, shopping, etc. But now you don't have to medicate yourself. You now have a power that is available to you 24 hours a day, 7 days a week. Use the fundamentals in this book to create your Power Belief System™ for health.

Power Belief Exercise

A nice exercise I created for general stress reduction is called "The vacuum cleaner". Use a comfortable technique to relax. Visualize yourself getting a new tape for you to record on and see yourself placing it in a recorder in your head. Now imagine a vacuum cleaner in your body with a light on the front. This vacuum cleaner's only job is to "vacuum" up stress that is above normal for you (beyond stress). Nothing can hide from this vacuum that is "beyond stress" because the light will find it! Visualize the vacuum sucking up the stress and notice how you start feeling better immediately. After the vacuum cleaner has finished, empty the bag into the air and notice that all the particles of stress disintegrate and harm no one else. Your tape has been recording this positive experience for you to use at a later time. You can get so good at this exercise that simply saying the command, "vacuum", to yourself can initiate relaxation!

Chronic Pain

The second domain of health I would like to focus on is chronic pain. I've done most of my training and research in this area and it still amazes me how strong our mind-body connection really is. Chronic pain is perhaps one of the most complex areas of health that I have studied. It accounts for countless days of work absences and is the third leading cause of disability in the United States.

It's important to distinguish chronic pain from acute pain. Acute pain is caused when you hit your thumb with a hammer, pull too many weeds and strain your back or play football on the weekend and work your muscles more than normal. You don't worry about the soreness and pain you are experiencing (although you may say a few choice words) because you know it will go away. It has before. But what if it didn't and your thumb that you hit with the hammer never quits throbbing? How would you feel? Would it affect your life in any way?

That is the world of chronic pain. The International Association for the Study of Pain defines pain as *"an unpleasant sensory and emotional experience associated with actual or potential tissue damage or*

69

described in terms of such damage." Chronic pain is defined as pain that persists longer than 6 months and results in the need for long-term treatment. Most of you know that pain in general is very complex and is comprised of many components. Chronic pain not only has a biological or physical component, but psychological and social components as well. The experience of pain includes sensory, emotional, behavioral and cognitive components. Chronic pain does <u>not</u> solely depend on tissue damage <u>and is not</u> necessarily related to it. This diversity of pain experiences has created difficulties in understanding the meaning of pain. Dennis Turk, Ph.D., noted pain psychologist and researcher, allowed us to see pain as more of a perception involving the individual's awareness, concept and appraisal of pain. This perception, in turn, is impacted by the individual's definition of pain based on personal attitudes and expectations over time. Consequently, the extent of pain, suffering and disability is associated with an interpretive process and not just the degree of tissue damage. As efforts to treat pain have paralleled the way pain is conceptualized and evaluated, clinically effective models of chronic pain have evolved, expanding the definition of pain.

It's just recently in western medicine that we have realized that patients who go in for pain treatment not only need a comprehensive medical assessment, but also require a comprehensive psychological assessment that evaluates what the patients' beliefs, attitudes, expectations and rules are about their condition. What coping strategies does the patient use? What adjustments have they had to make in their lives because of their pain? Did you know that only within the past few years have hospitals been mandated to ask about patients' pain levels? Pain is now the fifth vital sign. It is remarkable that we are now starting to realize that it is the patients' belief systems that can affect their perceived level of pain. I say perceived because we can't measure how much pain a person is in. They have to tell us.

Chronic Pain and Your Belief System

I would like to begin this section describing two previous clients of mine that suffered from chronic lower back pain. Clients John and Richard both have herniated disks at the same level. A herniation is the outcome of having the pulpous material (gel like substance) protrude from between our vertebra. The purpose of this pulpous material is to create a cushion for the disks to sit on and acts like a shock absorber. Without it you have disk on disk. Herniations can be quite painful and can affect how you do certain activities in your life (e.g. lifting, walking, sitting or sleeping.). Sometimes this pulpous material will shoot out at the surrounding nerves causing more pain. The pain is sometimes relieved by surgery, but surgery could cause other problems.

John and Richard have both suffered herniations from a work related injury caused by lifting boxes. I was always amazed at how these two gentlemen with the same

71

injury, the same health status and no previous surgeries could be so different in their perception of their pain condition. John was almost completely disabled by his pain, and Richard was still active, working and exercising. So, why were they at such opposite levels of functioning? You can answer this by now, right? Let's list several factors that would perpetuate pain disability:

- Physical conditioning and reconditioning
- Inappropriate use of medications
- Lack of job skills
- Emotional factors
- Beliefs about their pain

For example, if you were in poor shape before the accident, it might be harder to get where you need to be physically to rehabilitate after the injury. If you don't get the physical therapy that is recommended, you are setting yourself up for failure. In addition, you might say, "I can only do one thing. I can move boxes. That is ALL I know how to do!" You perceive that have no other job skills. You are now suffering symptoms of sadness, grief, nervousness and hopelessness. If you had some of these symptoms before the injury, they are now worse. Your beliefs about your pain may be telling you, "I will never be able to function again. I am useless to my family. Why try? It won't help."

I wanted to find out why John and Richard were functioning so differently, so I chose to study this phenomenon for my research for my Ph.D. My research investigated what types of pain specific attitudes or beliefs are related to the way people adjust to chronic pain. The literature in the area reported that people with chronic pain who endorsed negative attitudes or had belief systems related to more perceived disability would report greater dysfunction in different areas of their life than people who endorsed attitudes related to lesser or no perceived disability. So my research investigated the responses on an instrument that surveyed peoples' attitudes about their pain and looked for correlations (patterns) between how these people perceived themselves functioning in certain areas such as physical, psychosocial and independent areas of care. In other words, what beliefs, attitudes, expectations, etc. (belief system) were they endorsing and because of this endorsement, at what level of functioning would they perceive themselves? Other studies have shown that people who perceive that they have low levels of control over their pain and perceive themselves as disabled (negative tapes) associate with higher levels of dysfunction in different areas of their lives. What I found in my research was that people who endorsed negative attitudes about their pain reported that they perceived themselves as more disabled and felt more hopeless over their situation! So again it comes down to the belief system.

John was to the point of using a walker, and Richard was preparing to go hiking in Hawaii. They were so interesting to study because they were so similar in most areas (age, family, finances, etc.) but were producing such different outcomes! The difference is how they perceived themselves and what they visualized as their future. John had a belief system that was really negative and had tapes that were saying things like "You are a screw up just like your daddy. Nothing is visibly wrong with you. You are just a baby. You are not a man anymore. You can't even satisfy your wife." He had a family that was not supportive and pressured him daily to go back to work. John told me that his daughter said that he had gotten hurt on purpose so he wouldn't have to buy her the things she wanted. She told John that it was not fair that all of her friends had fathers that were productive, and he was embarrassing her! Unfortunately, I hear this too often. Many people who suffer from chronic pain don't know how to use their inner resources, and they just give up.

John was very skeptical about working with me concerning his chronic pain. He was just getting used to coming to our sessions and venting, and he felt that was all he could do. I challenged John, and he began to learn how to relax in much the same way I described in Chapter 3. He began to notice that while he was relaxing and using visualization, he was not hurting. He started to be honest with himself about what tapes were playing in his head and actually started to realize the source. We started loading his brain with positive and productive tapes. I gave John a prescription to practice his relaxation and visualization three times a day. When we met, we loaded his brain with positive tapes of healing, happiness

74

and reduced pain intensity. We then cemented these tapes in with visualization and relaxation.

After about a month, John said to me sheepishly, "Doc, I have a confession. This stuff really works, and I have been doing my exercises all day long." I asked what that was doing for him. John then started to cry and said, "My pain levels are as low as they have ever been, and sometimes I truly have no pain!" I asked him what he thought was happening? John replied, "I'm not sure, but my wife is even noticing." John was creating his Power Belief System™.

Richard was the complete opposite to John. When I asked him why he was functioning so well, he replied, "Because that is what I want, and I have always gotten what I wanted." He went on to explain to me that he had used what he called "picturing" since he was a kid, and he gave this technique credit for his perceived success in life. He said he could "feel" he would be all right even if he couldn't do the same work. He said, "I'll just get retrained in something else!" Richard was certainly the epitome of the Power Belief System™.

How strong are our beliefs? I can answer this by sharing an Internet article (WebMD Health, July 10, 2002) I read recently that described the effects of a study on placebo surgery in patients with arthritis of the knee. The study reported that one group of patients was treated just as successfully with a small incision and nothing else (placebo) as those who had the complete arthroscopic operation. The placebo patients believed the surgery had been performed, and the surgeon informed them the surgery was successful. The patients believed this and were able to achieve relief. This was a powerful conclusion in this study!

A concrete example of how our brains can't tell the difference between fact and fantasy can be seen in brain scans of individuals that were asked to imagine images and then actually view images (pictures). These brain scans have shown that looking at a picture of a tree or simply imagining a tree will produce activity in the same area of the brain. In another example, athletes who sat for two weeks and imagined shooting hoops improved their free-throw scores as much as those who physically shot hoops. They were actually going through the motions, and they believed and felt that they were shooting hoops. This is really powerful stuff! There have also been reports that have shown that significant gains in muscle strength can be realized by just imaging doing repetitive tasks even though muscles did not physically move.

So just understanding the implications of how our thoughts can create different changes in the physiological processes of our body is powerful in itself. What do you think the implication would be if our belief systems were saying stuff like, "I am worthless, I will never get pregnant or this cancer is going to kill me"? Why is it so easy for us to understand that these negative thoughts can impact us in a negative way, but we are so resistant to believing the positive ones can have the same power? I truly believe that the simple most important factor for predicting lifelong good health and longevity is how we think. How do my beliefs affect my health? What am I telling myself? Why would I have beliefs that create negative health? Is there something I am getting out of negative health? It may be hard to realize, but you have to ask yourself whether there are some perceived benefits you get from being ill? "Maybe I will not get the attention that I have gotten if I am healthy." "Maybe I will have to stand on my own." These are the negative tapes you must identify. Is there anything in your history that might be affecting your health system behavior? What affirmations are you using? Using your Power Belief System™ gets to the root of the cause and allows change to be initiated by loading your brain with thoughts of wellness and health!

Pitfalls

When you are creating your Power Belief System™ using the techniques in this book, always be aware of what limiting beliefs you may have about the techniques themselves. For example some people have told me that if they learn to relax too much they will not be sharp in the work they do. This is not true. Learning to relax and become aware of your thoughts will only make your work sharper. You won't be giving away your energy to nonproductive thoughts, and you will have more energy for the work you want to do. You are in control of everything you do. You will never be in a situation with

77

relaxation where you will not be aware of anything you should be aware of (smoke, baby crying, etc). You will actually become more aware of these things, but at a different level than before. Your brain will multitask. Remember your brain will take care of your breathing and heartbeat without any help from you. However, you have the option of adding quality control to these functions; for example, how you are breathing and how fast your heart is beating.

Health concerns occupy a great deal of our thoughts, time and resources. It may be difficult for any of us to accept that we may have had a part in creating or maintaining ill health. The irony of this is that most of us have difficulty accepting good health! We engage in negative behaviors that create dissonance in our stated goals of good health. We are then surprised when we experience the effects of those negative behaviors. We now have a Power Belief System™ that gives US the control over our thoughts, choices and behaviors. The reality is that you may always have the condition you are struggling with, but you do not have to suffer because of it! Your well-being is at stake here. I define well-being as living the life you want despite any health obstacles. You can see, from the examples in this chapter, that your perception of whether you are ill or healthy determines your outcomes and well-being. Your Power Belief System™ may not cure your disease, but it will allow you to live a wonderful life in spite of it. The content of your belief system is the greatest factor in determining lifelong good health and longevity! Using your power of choice is the most potent medicine of all!

As It Applies to Health

7

YOUR POWER BELIEF SYSTEM™
AS IT APPLIES TO WORK

*"Always bear in mind, that your own resolution
to succeed is more important than any other
thing."* Abraham Lincoln

No matter what business or level of an organization you work in, you may struggle with the same problems we all do:

- Balance between work and life
- Managing the resources you have at work
- Trying to work in and at something you love

Many times we are caught up in the endless cycle of working more hours for more money. As we earn more money, our expenses usually increase, so we need to make more money by working more hours, etc. Our family and social lives may suffer because we are always working. How many times have you seen companies outsource jobs because they feel that labor is cheaper in another country? These companies do not see humans as resources or having any tangible value. Have you ever heard someone say, "It's not my life; it's just a paycheck." Have you noticed that earning this paycheck consumes most of your waking hours? How can something that requires so much of your time not be important to you? Don't you think you may be limiting yourself by thinking this way? In this chapter, we look at these important issues of work-life balance, resource management and loving our work and how using your Power Belief System™ can help you be efficient in all three areas.

Work-Life Balance

In a leadership conference, a poll was taken about what people needed in their employment, what would make them happy and what would make them more successful? Ninety-one percent of the people attending the conference said that they thought the business world needs a greater consciousness, more integrity and to be more caring so we all could achieve balance and fulfillment in their lives.

One of the main things that people struggle with, males or females, is finding balance and harmony in our work and personal lives. As business people we experience conflict between giving ourselves wholeheartedly to our careers in order to climb the ladder of success and spending time with our families and living the "good" life. Most of us are not successful at managing career and family because we perceive there is not enough time in the day to do both. But if you step back and look at things through the lens of your Power Belief System™ you can see how you can start making choices to obtain the life you desire. Harmony and balance are very important because without them, we will not function at peak levels of performance. The skills we gain by using the Power Belief System™ enable us to bring ourselves back to equilibrium. If we recall from the last chapter on health, ignoring symptoms of imbalance can result in many stress related symptoms. Symptoms such as headache, gastrointestinal, anxiety and depression can interfere with our work efficiency and create even more stress for us.

Jan was a client who sought help after she became physically exhausted in her business and began losing clients because of her inefficiency. Jan owned a small business consulting firm that competed with much larger companies. She was the sole employee of her company. She even felt it was important for her to answer her own phones when potential customers called. She insisted on doing every detail of a job because she could not trust anyone to do the job as well as her. In the beginning, this was a good model for her, and she was able to keep up. However, as she began to receive more work, her efficiency dropped off considerably.

She was working all the time, not sleeping or resting well and was starting to develop severe stress headaches. Her relationship of several years fell apart because she felt she didn't have the time to invest in it. She told herself that once she was successful, she would pursue her personal life! Jan was at her wits end with all of her responsibilities, and her reputation was at stake. At the time she saw me, she had not returned phone calls from the previous day, which was suicide in her business. Jan's headaches were getting worse and she was having trouble concentrating and starting to panic that she would lose her business. I was able to convince Jan to hire someone to answer the phones temporarily until she could devise a plan of action.

Jan began the process of trying to identify her current belief system. This was hard for her because she initially felt this as a waste of time and that she should be working. I asked her what it would cost in sales to her business if she did nothing. Jan agreed she needed to do this work so she could create her Power Belief System™ and save her business. She discovered that she was playing tapes that said she was a failure. She would never complete anything, and she could never live up to her family's expectations. Jan also started to realize that she "ran" her romantic relationships the same as her business. She was always afraid of someone leaving her in the beginning of the romance, and she began to create this state of abandonment through the negative tapes she was playing.

Jan was able to learn a relaxation technique that allowed her to continue identifying her current belief system. The movie screen technique was especially helpful with her inner visioning. To initiate the chaos she needed to make positive changes, Jan visualized a magnet running over her negative tapes and erasing them. Jan started to record new tapes that told her that she was a smart person and it was OK to delegate some of her everyday tasks to someone else. She recorded tapes that said she was creative and responsible for the early growth of her business and by delegating some of her task she would be able to concentrate on growing the business even more.

She allowed herself to visualize her "perfect office" with a receptionist and even an associate. She visualized her family being supportive of her. She visualized herself entering a healthy relationship. She allowed herself 15 minutes a day for these visualizations. Within a short time, she started to feel better, and her headaches were becoming less frequent. She created a book for herself where she placed pictures that represented new clients for her business. Jan created her Power Belief System™ and was creating a healthy business and life for herself. She also created opportunities for her new receptionist through the ripple effect of her new powerful belief system.

Although I think these principles are important for everyone involved in business activities, they ring especially important for entrepreneurs and people who own their own businesses, like Jan. Entrepreneurs and business owners carry tremendous responsibility on their own shoulders. Depending on external conditions, their businesses may be affected by economic conditions more than large businesses where the ripple effect of environmental and outside concerns take longer to affect a single employee. Not only do entrepreneurs and business owner make choices based on their belief system, but they may also buy into their customer's belief systems as well. They may struggle more with cognitive dissonance in order to make a sale. This creates more stress and all the problems associated with stress. It is vital that self-employed business people create and use their Power Belief System™. Like everything I talk about, the bottom line is your perception and beliefs.

> *"Believe that life is worth living and your belief will help create the fact."*   William James

Managing Resources

The way we learn to handle business here in the Western world is to learn the policies and procedures of the company, the games played and, if you're lucky, the rules to the game. If you are eyeing a top position, you may even get to know the likes and dislikes of the person that you are trying to impress. Companies promote much competition among employees both in times of feast and famine.

A client, who was in upper management at the time, told me that he knew everything about his company and where they wanted to be, but he knew nothing of the people. He said at times he even thought that most people might be expendable and that the majority of what they did could be automated or outsourced at a lower price, so that's just what he did. He outsourced a customer service portion of his business to a company in another country. He told me that everything they did was scripted. It would be a big cost savings for the company and would bring him the admiration from the "higher-ups" whom he wanted to impress.

Well it did bring him notoriety...and a "pink slip". He didn't take the time to see the human element in his decision or the problems his customers would face in speaking to people from another culture and language. He was only thinking of himself, and the "higher-ups" only saw the bottom line - saving money! He contacted me after losing his job and wanted to know why and how this could have happened.

When we started working together to see the makeup of his current belief system, we found all kinds of skeletons in his system. He was telling himself all kinds of negative and destructive things, most of which he had loaded from adolescence. He had a belief that he was only worth something if he could be a CEO, and that people not at this level were merely rungs on a ladder for his climb to the top. After all, that's what his dad did. His dad was never home and, when he was, he was always looking for ways to be more efficient and save his company money. He perceived his dad as always being rewarded for his work and that his mom and siblings should be proud and understanding. Emotion, his dad taught him, had no place in the workplace. My client had done a great job of modeling and living the life of his dad.

Taking this a step further, if you are in management, your core belief system is affecting what you do, and it is also affecting how you treat the people you work with. This will affect their belief system as well, and it will affect their family's belief systems. Get the picture?

Imagine the people who report to you having positive outcomes and reaching their goals because this will help you as well (that energy thing). Walk down the hall and feel the excitement of working with a group of talented people that love what they do even if that hasn't been true in the past. It's time for intervention, for chaos, and for you to start seeing the change!

We don't have to limit our conversation to the individual employee: a company has a belief system as well. Basically, when we are looking at it from the system point of view, we must determine what makes the organization tick. What does the organization want to achieve and is that in line with your beliefs and your own goals? From a systems perspective, is it not better for us to involve everyone in the organization's goal setting? Doesn't it make sense for everyone to be empowered to achieve? Think about the "ripple effect" this would have. Like energy attracts like energy.

Also consider the perceptions you automatically have about people that work with you? Does it matter if they are male or female? Does it matter if they are a different race or ethnicity? What if they went to an Ivy League school? Those are the things that you should review when you are building your fundamentals (Chapters 2 and 3). Business is nothing but a series of different relationships that you have on a daily basis. Most of us are in those business relationships more than we are in our family relationships. We spend over 40 hours a week with business associates, and we must examine in detail what our perceptions (beliefs) are about these associates.

What belief system do you have now that's affecting how you get business or how you operate within your business? Using your Power Belief System™ enables you to work with any group of people (no matter what your differences are), see opportunities in everything and develop good solutions. You are confident enough to ask for help from successful people that have had similar goals. You do not envy your associates anymore. You use their strengths as opportunities for growth. You don't have to scratch and claw your way though business. When you are looking from the system level, you realize there is enough for everyone!

> *"People only see what they are prepared to see"*
> Ralph Waldo Emerson.

Love What You Do

When you are discovering your power belief system related to business, you need to ask yourself what the truth is in achieving this business success. Is this really what I want to do? Am I doing this because I think I need to do it and this is what is expected of me? Is this what my father and mother did, and I'm just following in their footsteps?

> *"There is no scarcity of opportunity to make a living at what you love to do, there is only scarcity of resolve to make it happen"* Dr. Wayne Dyer.

89

You have to do what you love and love what you do. If you are someone that is not "doing what you love", then you are not using the power you have available to you. Create your Power Belief System™ so that you will have a multitude of choices in business and in life. Use the techniques of inner visioning to find out your heart's desire. If you do not possess the skills necessary to achieve your heart's desire, then surround yourself with people who do and allow them to help you through this transformation. Set your sights on returning to school to achieve the skills you need. Nothing is impossible when you load your brain with what you want. Now act as if you already posses what you want and watch what happens!

There will always be conflicts related to what you are trying to achieve, especially in business. This is part of the cycle of life in business. It doesn't mean that you can't succeed when there is some other person to contend with. You just have to be in your Power Belief Zone™ so you can recognize and handle the challenges.

Your job does not have to be a chore or an unpleasant task. Do you wake up in the morning thinking I hate this job? Do you find yourself thinking, "I'd do anything else rather than this job, but I'm married to this paycheck, so I have to go to work?" What do you think these kinds of tapes will create for you? Besides, you are probably not doing the best job you could do because you hate what you are doing.

Pitfalls

If you are telling yourself that you are not going to make it in the business world, that you are going to go bankrupt, that you will always be at the same level, then that is what will happen. We are excellent at producing negative results! Some people have a business work schedule that is flexible and allows them time to strengthen their Power Belief System™ and create more positive and productive tapes. Why don't these people take advantage of this? If you are one of these people, what do you do with your free time? Watch TV? KILL time? How many people have said that? Aren't you worth investing in yourself? If you have an extra 10 minutes a day, you can use that time to visualize success and load your brain with positive and productive thoughts! Why don't you? Are you too tired? You just want to relax and NOT THINK. Does that really happen, not thinking? NO, it does not.

When you are not being productive you will go back to your old tapes (thinking) and reinforce them in your down time. Remember, it's easy to go back to the old stuff. We can do it instantly and unconsciously. Try what I am suggesting. In your free 10 minutes (even in the restroom) use the visualization from the quick shower exercise (Chapter 4). Think about what you want to accomplish this week and start setting goals for the future. Feed your brain the good stuff!

"The beginning is the most important part of the work." Plato.

What do you truly believe about your success? Are you sabotaging yourself at the beginning of a project so you will not achieve success? How is your history impacting your ability to achieve success? What tapes are you playing? Maybe you have had situations where you did not achieve success, and you are now saying, "I did not succeed before, so I am not going to succeed now." Maybe you are thinking that your father and mother reached a certain level of employment, and you can't go farther than them. Remember the client that had trouble making more money than her father? What affirmations are you telling yourself that are not working for you? And what are they actually affirming?

The main limitation that people have is their belief system. Their perceptions of reality are based on these belief systems. Your belief system acts as a filter and leads you to make certain choices. People will always pay attention to what they feel is important and ignore what is not. What is important is encoded in your belief system! You have to know what you are planting in your foundation (belief system) before you can cultivate choices; otherwise, you will not know the difference between a weed and a flower!

Summary

Everything we do, every choice we make, is governed by our belief system. It doesn't matter if it is personal, business or health related. The only way to make positive choices so they will ripple through all of your life (work, personal, etc.) is to change those negative and ineffective tapes at the core of your being.

You also need to ask yourself what picture you think you are sending out to your employees, boss, colleagues, or customers? What picture are you sending out of yourself? You can only produce a picture that you can see! Are you sending out a confident picture, one that's creative and has lots of ideas? One that gets along with other people and thinks outside the box? One that's a good mediator? Or, are you sending out a picture that says I'm really hesitant to do business with you, and I'm really shaky about what I'm doing here?

Always do a reality check to determine what you are really saying to people, even subconsciously. What are you feeling when you are around these people? What are you feeling when you're working on this project? What body signals are you getting? Do you get heartburn, or is your stomach upset? Are you getting headaches? Do you clench your jaws? Do you feel sleepy? Are you irritated? Are you angry? Are you critical of people in your group? This is all wonderful data that you can use when creating your Power Belief System™. Put your mind on the work you want to do and load your brain with these thoughts.

Ask yourself, "If I remove all obstacles, what kind of work do I want to do?" Where do you see yourself 6 months from now, five years from now? Are you reality checking everything so you know that you are using your Power Belief System™? For example, if your goal is to be a CEO, and you have made a personal commitment to work 50-60 hours a week to turn the company around, is your family agreeable? If not, you will have cognitive dissonance, and you run the risk of failing because you have put yourself into a situation that is a no-win – no-win.

Conflicts in general are important enough to discuss in the next chapter.

8

YOUR POWER BELIEF SYSTEM™
AS IT APPLIES TO CONFLICT

*H*ow do we define conflict? Webster defines conflict as:

1. To be in opposition; contend; clash.

2. A struggle for mastery; battle.

3. An opposition or clash as of beliefs, interests, etc.

You can't escape conflict; it's all around us. It's natural and it's part of that synergy, if you will, that I refer to as chaos. Conflict originates in many different ways, as do our reactions. We may react with aggression, denial, sadness or resistance.

Our reaction to conflict could be a response to the way we were taught, the blueprint of our belief systems, the way mom and dad responded to conflict or the way we responded to conflict with siblings. We may have suppressed our reactions in different environments. But if you were pushed hard enough, aggression and negativity may have been the way you reacted! Sometimes, these conflicts get us into trouble because we really don't know how to resolve them. But if you think about it, why are you always the one having the conflict? Your buddies and friends never seem to have as much conflict. They seem to be able to handle things without conflict. Things that "press your buttons" don't press theirs. We are all individuals, so we are going to have certain things press

<u>our</u> buttons and not anyone else's. You might ask yourself the following questions:

- What is it about the conflict in my life?
- Why do I need this conflict?
- Am I creating this conflict?
- How are my history, my learned behavior and my belief system affecting the way I go about handing or resolving conflict?
- How do I manage or mismanage these conflicts?

It all has to do with, of course, your belief system! It all has to do with the tapes that you have playing in your head because the tapes show us how to react (choices) and what to do (behaviors) in different types of situations. The essence of resolving conflict has actually been a running theme throughout the book.

Conflicts appear in our health, business, communications, relationships and even our faith, so we are not going to avoid them. But we need to realize what the core problems are and how to resolve them. Now that you are using your Power Belief System™, you can sit back and really look at the types of conflicts you've had in your life and how you have gone about resolving or not resolving them. You can also see how you have knee-jerk responses to some of your conflicts.

Think about the last time that you might have had some difficulty or conflict with your significant other. Perhaps it was over a credit card bill or the way that you were disciplining your children. Maybe you have silently been worried about the family's finances. You look at this month's credit card statement and before you even take a breath you might have screamed, "What is this bill for? I thought we were going to try to save money!" How did that work for you? What did it accomplish? It probably created tension and stress for the other person, and they might have reacted the same way you taught them to react. The same way they taught you to react by raising their voice, and this never really solves anything. Without the complete knowledge of the situation (not available during knee-jerking), you would not know if the bill was something that you both had agreed on that you just forgot about!

You know that any conflict that you handle like the example above won't solve anything unless you see this as the chaos you need to move yourself (and your significant other – ripple effect) in a different direction. You know one of the reasons that we have difficulty with conflict is because we are associating conflict with a negative implication. Conflict doesn't necessarily have to be negative. The same is true for chaos; it doesn't have to be negative. Chaos can also be positive because it produces the change that you need in certain areas of your life. We can see that it is the same concerning conflict. If I say the word conflict, people think of a lot of negative images (for example, physical and verbal fights). But there are many peaceful things that happen during conflict, too. Think about peace movements in general and people marching for civil rights. Those are conflicts as well, but our perception may be totally different. Why? Maybe because we may see a value in these movements.

The only way we can get past our knee-jerk reaction to conflict is to use our Power Belief System™ which teaches us to relax during situations of conflict and really try to look at the core situation. Ask yourself: What tape am I playing or what trigger is setting off another tape to play? Why is this upsetting me? No one is saying not to stand up for yourself, speak your heart or stand up for your beliefs. I am not saying that at all! Though you do have to get calm and into yourself to be able to truly realize what is happing. You have to ask yourself, "Am I standing up for what I believe? Or is this person or situation really just causing a tape to play in my head?" Perhaps the situation is kicking off a tape you haven't played in a while! You may be thinking that although you have done a lot of work to get to a point where you feel better about most of your tapes, you still have this one trigger in your life that you need to work on and remove. When we are able to relax and start looking at the core issues, things start making sense. We are now looking at things from a larger perspective; a holistic way of looking at the issues. We start to realize that we are not in conflict with another human or situation but with how they perceive the situation of conflict with us!

The greatest thing about our Power Belief System™ is that we have the choice to be in our Power Belief Zone™

anytime we want. Using the fundamentals in Chapters 2 and 3, we are able to relax and become aware and focused and realize the core issue of what is really happening in this conflict situation. We have a choice everyday and every single moment to be centered. When we are not centered and certain conflicts happen that are causing negative tapes to play, we need, at that point, to start focusing on finding out what the heck is going on. This way we will be able to handle the conflict now and any similar conflict in the future.

Your perception of issues will change. Some issue that you once considered full of conflict will not be perceived as such when you are using your Power Belief System™. You may begin to realize that the conflict may not be a personal attack on you. Maybe it's a tape the other person is playing inside their head! But you need to know what it is about the other person's tape that is kicking off one of yours to play. So again, you have to be able to choose to be centered and focused and use the new blueprint of your belief system. Using your Power Belief System™ is exercising your power of choice that you are able to use every minute in every situation.

If you think about some examples in life where you've had some response to conflict, you can see how conflict (when perceived as negative) can really limit you and make you feel "stuck" in life. You may be thinking everything is cool, but here is this one thing that you can't let go of. Conflict in itself is an opportunity to look inside ourselves and see exactly what we have in our belief system that needs to change; what we need to load our brain with to create new tapes for positive change. We have to deal with conflict effectively. We have to achieve a balance in life through choice, and we have to understand what true power we have and continue to cultivate that power using our Power Belief System™. By doing this we will break though this mediocre life with mediocre successes into a life with excellent successes that we deserve and are put here to have!

Conflict Resolution

The goal of conflict resolution is to tear apart the conflict itself, look at the true content, find out why it is adversarial and determine why this conflict is doing what is does to you. It's not the other person that you are having trouble with. It's not the company. It's not this, and it's not that. It's you! Now we have been looking at conflict and learning how to change our knee-jerk responses into an opportunity for growth. Turn your adversary into a partner. You will hear yourself saying, "This person has something to teach me. I don't have a problem with this person; it's the message. It's the content that is causing a tape to play in my head, and that should be my focus!" Turn this conflict into strength and power. Listen to all sides. There may be something this person is suggesting that you perceive in a way that's allowing negative tapes to start playing, and that makes you uncomfortable. It may create the perceptions of lack and hopelessness, and those perceptions are what you need to look at. Conflict and the stress we produce are both neutral things. It's our reaction and our response to the conflict that is causing the difficulties. Whatever outcome from conflict we experience, we created and chose. No one and no situation can make us feel anything we are not allowing ourselves to feel!

> *"Your own mind is a sacred enclosure into which nothing harmful can enter except by your permission"* Ralph Waldo Emerson.

Using conflict more as an opportunity to grow, rather than a win or lose process requires us to use our Power Belief System™ and figure out exactly what is going on. Conflict to me, as I mentioned earlier, is not any different than chaos. It's positive and negative. It depends on how you are viewing it. To me chaos/conflict is a motivator for change. For anything to change, not just in our species but any species, there has to be some movement. There has to be some chaos, some challenge. Conflict creates one of the best growth opportunities. The problem is that when we see it, our perception is so negative that we internalize. We walk away, and we haven't done anything but create another stress situation for ourselves. We also have created a whole new series of tapes to play when situations like this arise. You have to be willing to realize what response you are having to the conflict.

Pay attention to what is happening to your body during conflict. Usually people want to fight, run away or freeze up. What's happening to you? What are you feeling? Is your skin tingling? Is your heart beating fast? Is your face flushed? Are you gritting your teeth? Are you scared? Are you thinking "Oh, my gosh. They are going to find out what I am really made of?" Sometimes we don't even realize that what is happening is conflict. We are so good at denial. We have all of these bodily reactions, but when you ask us to label the reactions, we don't label them as conflict. But it is conflict, and we have to be aware of that and acknowledge it. Accept the conflict for what it is and move to the next step. Whatever is happening, you have to get in tune with it so you can load your brain with a new tape. The next time you have a conflict try to first accept that it is conflict.

We are now willing to change and accept new ideas because we know that everything that happens to us is an opportunity for growth. Now we have tapes that are playing an opposite message. You realize that you don't have any buttons to press anymore. You realize there is something in your perception that may be different or something in the other person's perception that may be different and this is an opportunity for me to grow and change. Change will happen for the other person too (ripple). That is the way we have to look at this! We do have to find that special state where are centered, focused and aware so we can realize that this conflict (although we may not use this label anymore) is an opportunity for growth.

The Zone

Think about professional athletes that play basketball, tennis and other sports. Think about a tennis match at break point. It's a win or lose point. The athlete has to be very centered and focused. Now understand that this is a conflict. If the athlete is to give into the conflict and not see it as an opportunity for growth and change, she will lose. If the athlete gets centered and really starts using her Power Belief System™ to see that she needs to adjust her play, she will begin to believe she will win. She is in her Power Belief Zone™!

Most people believe that these types of skills are only available to elite people that train and practice and this "Zone" is some special gift they have. It is not a special gift. It is available to every one of us! You have a Power Belief System™ that is available to you 24 hours a day, 7 days a week. USE IT!

Romantic Relationships

One of the keys about conflict resolution you see in romantic relationships is that one partner in the relationship will hold all of their reactions to conflict inside where it just builds up. Then one day a word (usually benign) from one partner sets off an explosion in the other partner that was holding everything in. This person that internalizes conflict, records on her tape what she would do or say when she is in a conflict and keeps adding to this tape every time another conflict arises. Finally they hit the end of the tape and KABOOM. They explode! Of course the explosion doesn't solve anything, and the other person is usually thinking, "Where did that come from? Why didn't you tell me you were feeling this way?" At this point no one in the relationship knows what is going on.

Pitfalls

Everybody gets upset about things, but you don't have to use anger or aggression against another person. Again, conflict is a way for you to grow and a way for you to explore. Maybe you will explore and realize that this is not a person you want to be with or a company you want to work for or a business venture you want to pursue. That's OK! Think about all the conflicts you have had in your life. When do you settle things? When do things finally to come to pass and you are able to sit down, talk and find a solution? It is not during the time when you are screaming and yelling and making accusations. It is during the times when you are calm, focused and aware, and you say to the person "I want to hear you. I want to know what you are saying. Let's talk about this." This happens when you let go of all that other stuff and get down to the core. What is causing your negative tapes to play? That's when you find the resolution.

So during moments of conflict when you start to feel anger and other negative emotions, ask yourself "What can I learn about dealing with future situations like this? How can I make sure that I don't get stuck in this type of problem again?" This kind of positive approach gives you a productive way to deal with what has happened. It leads you into learning something about how to deal better with these types of situations in the future. You don't have to feel like all of this is a waste of time because you know this is an opportunity for growth and realization for you. You can transform this conflict and anger into something very positive. Why? Because it is energy. Remember energy is energy! Depending on the way you look at it, it can be positive or negative. So why waste your time with this anger or negative energy. Why not change it into something positive that is going to pump you up. Change it into a growth experience. Change it into an awareness that is going to fill you and replenish your energy.

Using the Techniques

There may be a lot of fear involved when a conflict arises, and you may not even be aware of the fear. That's why, by using your Power Belief System™, you are able to get into yourself and start questioning your core beliefs and find out what is going on. There are many different techniques you can use (Chapter 3). For example, use visualization and imagine yourself being able to talk to a person that you perceive difficulties with. Imagine being able to ask them all kinds of questions. You will be surprised at the answers you get because you are focusing on you. This is a simple technique you can use.

If something is too stressful for you to imagine, and it is creating negative body sensations then use the "movie screen" technique I detailed in Chapter 3. Get into a relaxed position and project your thoughts out onto a screen that you are simply watching like you are watching a movie. You can comment on this movie. You can watch all the detail, but you are not experiencing any of it. This will let you run through what is going on, and you will be able to see certain patterns that are happening. Using this technique of the Power Belief System™, you can get to the core of the problem and see where your fears are coming from and how you can change those fears into success and growth for you! As you are doing this visualization you will realize that you have been learning how to read the signals from your body and mind using your Power Belief System™. So while you are doing this exercise and watching scenes on this movie screen, what is your body and mind telling you? Is your jaw tensing? Do you have butterflies in your stomach? Or are you feeling some warmness and maybe tingling on some part of your body? That's a good sign; the warmer our bodies are the more relaxed we are!

Summary

Conflict can cause knee-jerk reactions when we allow our faulty belief system, with its negative tapes, to color our perceptions of conflict. Conflict, through the lens of the Power Belief System™, is chaos and an opportunity for change and growth. Don't fear conflict. Use it for your own good!

As It Applies to Conflict

9

IT'S JUST THE BEGINNING!
PULLING IT ALL TOGETHER

Your Power Belief System™ is an overarching structure that encompasses principles on how to live your life. You now know that you are in control of what you input. You have become aware from reading this book that many factors contribute to how and why you input data into this structure we call our Power Belief System™. I have shown you how the principles of this technology are woven into every aspect of your life. The choices you make, based on your structure of beliefs, will determine what life you will lead! This is true even if you feel that your choices were taken away from you through childhood neglect and abuse or adult experiences of abuse or illness. It is now your time and universal gift and right to live a life of happiness, prosperity, and well-being! You no longer have to be a prisoner of your faulty belief system. You no longer have to live your life based on your destructive blueprint. You can change your life! I have experienced this change in my own life and have seen the ripple effect in my family and friends. I have seen clients who were on their last thread of hope change their lives and break the cycles of fear and pain. I know that you can do this too! We are all the same. We are just sparks of an all-encompassing energy called by many names.

Although I do not consider this book religious, it is very spiritual. Not because I set out for it to be but because there is no other way to create and describe this technology without a message of spirituality coming through. Faith plays an important role in our lives. Faith is no different from just believing in something. Faith produces beliefs, and beliefs (and believing) produce faith! Most of us take these faiths and beliefs for granted and never question them until we experience some chaos that forces us.

There is a story that I like to tell (source unknown) about a woman and her daughter cooking a roast together. They were getting ready to put the roast in the oven and the mother said, "Don't forget to cut off the bad end of the roast before you put it in the oven because that's what gives it flavor."

The daughter replied, "Why is that?"

The mother answered, "I don't know why, but your grandmother always did that when I was growing up, and the roast always turned out wonderful."

The daughter then asked her mother "Have you ever tried cooking a roast without cutting the end off?"

Her mom said. "Oh yes, and it's just horrible. Ask your father. It was so dry."

So the daughter followed the advice, and then called her grandmother to ask her what was accomplished by cutting off the end of the roast.

The grandmother replied, "It doesn't accomplish anything other than making the roast small enough to fit in my oven!" This is a wonderful example of belief and faith and the outcomes they can produce.

I remember reading an account of a cancer patient who was receiving treatment for his tumor in the early days of chemotherapy. His doctors told this gentleman that they had only one treatment left to try, and it was experimental but was showing some interesting results in studies so far. This man agreed to the treatment and decided to do some research on his own about the drug. He found to his delight the medical community thought this was the next wonder drug in cancer treatment, and people were investing heavily in the drug company's stock. The man, convinced he had made the right choice, was eagerly awaiting the results of tests to see the effect the drug was having on the cancer. To the doctor's amazement, this man's tumor was almost gone. This man went from depression and constant pain to living life again. Even more astonishing, on his next visit he was cancer free! His doctor told him that he only needed to come in every few months for a check up if he was feeling well.

The man was so excited that he surprised his wife with a trip to Europe to celebrate. While he was in Europe he saw an article in the paper about a failed cancer drug and the investors who lost millions. He read this with sorrow for the people receiving the drug and for the people who lost money. He then read at the end of the article that the same drug, marketed under a different name (his drug), was being tested in the United States. The stock and the drug were worthless. The man died the next day! This man initially believed the drug would have a positive affect on his cancer. When he read the medical community thought the drug was the next miracle drug, he believed and his faith only strengthened him. He had placed all of his belief in this drug, and his belief system had no choice but to produce the outcomes from his beliefs (cancer free). When he found out the drug was useless, his belief system was shattered and he began playing his old tapes that said he was going to die!

Throughout the book, I use the metaphor of audiotapes playing in our brains to describe the process of the inner dialogues we have with ourselves. This metaphor was meaningful to me and to my clients. Many have told me that this was easy for them to visualize. It's important for you to understand and practice the fundamentals of the technology. It's less important that you use the metaphor of tapes. Use any metaphor that is meaningful to you. That is the KEY! I have used the metaphor of planting seeds (loading your brain) in the garden of your mind and pulling out the weeds (negative thoughts) to promote change.

An elderly client of mine told me that he understood the technology, but was having trouble thinking of his thoughts as tapes. He told me that he didn't have that much experience with tapes. After working with him, I discovered that he loved to fish, so we used fishing as his metaphor. He knew that he could

112

catch certain fish (that he perceived as good catches) by using bait that would attract these fish. So we visualized his brain as an ocean of fish with good (positive thoughts) and bad (negative thoughts) fish. He was in control of what he caught (choices, outcomes) depending on what bait (loading his brain, energy) he was using. This proved to be an excellent exercise for him to use, and he was able to promote change in his life. He told me that he was taking his wife along on these "fishing trips" as well. So it doesn't matter what you use. Just use something that is meaningful to you. There is no wrong or right metaphor to use!

I have had clients ask me, "What if I do everything right and still fail?" My answer is simple. You can't fail if you do everything in the right way for you. The thing you must remember is that even though we are all energy, we manifest (produce outcomes) in different ways. We have different personalities, different ways of learning and problem solving and are at different levels of believing or not believing that we can change. These factors will affect your transformation. For some, these factors, will not slow them down, but for others change might appear painfully slow. It's OK if you do not notice benefit at the same time as someone else. It DOES NOT mean that you are a failure. Think about everything you now know!

I said in the beginning that if you think you will get nothing out of this book, it will not disappoint you. You may be at a level that is close to wanting change but not quite there yet. Your readiness will determine your outcome. How could this be different from everything else we have been talking about? It cannot! Don't give up. You are worth more than giving up! Invest in yourself and find someone who is an expert in the Power Belief System™ and let them lead you through this. Some people need a little more help than others, and that is OK! Take weight loss, for example. Some people can get a book on nutrition and lose weight and maintain on their own. Others need a more formal approach that may involve coaching or therapy. It's not a weakness! The weakness would be not doing ANYTHING at all!

Give yourself the opportunity to ask yourself hard questions without fear of retribution from yourself. Take away all the knowledge, guilt and fear you have given yourself and ask, "What do I believe in? What is important to me? What truly makes me happy? If I could do anything, what would it be?" Let yourself see your differences at one level of perception and your oneness at another level. Notice the threads that weave between these two perceptions. We are microcosms of an all-encompassing macrocosm of energy.

Think of yourself as a drop of water from the ocean. You have all the qualities of the ocean but on a smaller scale. Your direction in life at this level of perception is the same. Once we start adding to or taking from ingredients of the water drop, we start to change its appearance and it resembles the ocean less and less. However, the power of this is the entire ocean is still in the water drop, only our perception has changed! We now focus on differences as opposed to similarities. Are we much different from this? Don't we forget that we are made from the same energy as everything else? By the time we have loaded our brains with all of our negative and destructive thoughts, we no longer resemble this all-encompassing energy that only wants to be your supplier of life.

To get where you want to go, you must know where you are going and believe you can get there! The process of creating your Power Belief System™ is similar. If you start on a trip but don't have a destination in mind, your trip will more than likely be long, with many detours. It could be exciting and eye-opening, or it could be frustrating and hard, depending on how you look at it. The more you travel, the more, through trial and error, you will narrow down the places to visit. You will eventually end up at the place you will call your destination. This way of traveling would take a bit longer than say a trip where you knew the exact location of your destination and had a map of how to get there. Neither approach is right or wrong, but the latter will get you where you need to go a lot faster.

You may want to use this process of creating your Power Belief System™ as a journey with no particular timeline, or you may want to be very structured going into the process with a clear defined goal. It's your choice! You will come to believe what you want to achieve with either process. Believing and acting as if you have obtained your goal or desire before its physical manifestation is the fastest way to achieve success. I told you of this in the beginning of the book and refer to it as the "Fake it 'till you make it" technique. When you do this you are setting up a continuous positive feedback loop that is loading your brain with the fact that you have achieved your goal. The most powerful voice you can listen to is your OWN! You will believe your own voice over all others, and this is why the work necessary to create your new belief system is so important (refer to Chapters 2 and 3).

Many people will say, "Yes I believe this, and I believe that I can create the change I desire in my life," but during times of uncertainty and stress they fall back to their own negative belief system. You now have the knowledge that having one set of beliefs for one situation and an opposite set of beliefs for another situation is the equivalent of "one step forward and two steps back!" Think of what tapes play during these conflicts. This is not an effective way to create change. Do you remember that I said that it doesn't matter in the beginning if you believe or not, eventually change will be produced? That is still true, but, like the metaphor of taking the unstructured trip, it will take a while to change because you are sabotaging yourself along the way. If you put yourself into a loop of belief-disbelief you will be stuck, because whatever you accomplish you erase on the next loop of the tape. This may be exactly what you have been doing and why other techniques have not worked. If you believe one thing one time and another thing another time, why do you question the results you get in life? Your brain and the universe are only doing what they have been instructed to do!

> *"We cannot manifest love when we have a mental equivalent of hate in our hearts and minds"* Ernest Holmes, *The Science of Mind.*

When you create and use your Power Belief System™, you initiate change and start thinking differently. This leads you to make different life choices and execute different behaviors. The cycle of creation continues as long as you give it permission. The universe is on your side and will align and produce what you believe is true. You have proven this to yourself time and again. Just look at what you have received so far. There is no risk involved, but there is great reward!

> *"The greatness of an artist lies in the building of an inner world, and in the ability to reconcile this inner world with the outer"* Albert Einstein.

When you are using your Power Belief System™ the positive change that you experience will ripple through everything else in the universe, not just your own life. It's a domino effect. There is no other choice! Can you see what kind of absolute power that is? Can you imagine the world if we all did this. What a ping-pong game of positive thought that would be!

This is a technology that will help you see difficulties in your life as opportunities for power. This book has revealed to you how your inner attitudes or thinking affect your outer world or behaviors. If you utilize the techniques in this book, I know that you will change and the change will be greater than YOU could ever imagine. Remember, the universe is on your side! Isn't it worth a try? What do you have to lose? Only a life that is no longer serving you!

I know that you are NOW living your dreams. You should now know how important you are in the big picture of life and how your change will affect everyone and everything around you. You are an awesome power and have this gift of a Power Belief System™ available to you 24 hours a day, 7 days a week. You job is only to become aware of it. Whatever you can conceive mentally through thought, you have the power to bring into materialization.

> *"Things are ideas in form. What else could they be?"* Ernest Holmes,
> *The Science of Mind*

Know yourself and your power and practice these techniques until they become part of your daily life and happen automatically like breathing and blinking your eyes. Believe in believing and watch miracles happen!

Therefore I say unto you, whatever things you ask when you pray, believe that you receive them, and you will have them." Mark 11:24

Pulling It All Together

More Information

More information on Dr. Gonzales and Health Psychology Services can be found at DrVeraGonzales.com.

We'd love to hear from you if you have a comment about the book or would like to share your experiences with the Power Belief System™. Go to PowerBeliefSystem.com where you will find a book forum to post comments, or you can email Dr. Gonzales directly at Dr-G@PowerBeliefSystem.com.